THE RUINED CITIES OF CEYLON

THE RUINED CITIES
OF
CEYLON

HENRY W. CAVE

Illustrated with Photographs taken by the Author in the year 1896

THIRD EDITION

GYAN

Published by

Gyan Publishing House
5, Ansari Road
Daryaganj, New Delhi-110002
Phone: 011-47034999, 9811692060
E-mail: books@gyanbooks.com

Distribution Network
gyanbooks.com
India, USA, Canada, UK, Australia, France

ISBN : 978-81-212-3973-8 (PB)
First Published, London, 1897

2nd Impression 2020

Printed at: Gyan Press, Delhi.

The Ruined Cities of Ceylon
Author: Henry W. Cave

THE RUINED CITIES OF CEYLON

BY

HENRY W. CAVE, M.A., F.R.G.S.

Member of the Royal Asiatic Society

AUTHOR OF "PICTURESQUE CEYLON," "GOLDEN TIPS," ETC.

Illustrated with Photographs taken by the Author in the year 1896

THIRD EDITION

LONDON

HUTCHINSON & CO

PATERNOSTER ROW

1904

ROCK TEMPLE AT DAMBULLA.

PREFACE TO NEW EDITION.

The public has called for a cheap edition of my "Ruined Cities of Ceylon." This is, of course, gratifying to me; but it is with some regret that I find myself compelled to adopt a different process of illustration in order to cheapen the work. I trust, however, that the collotypes here used will be found adequate for the purpose of giving a realistic idea of the present state of the ruins.

I have introduced three additional illustrations of work which has been completed since my first edition was published. For one of these, the Buddhist railing at Anuradhapura, I am indebted to Mr. Arthur E. Scovell; and for the others to Mr. W. L. H. Skeen. With these exceptions the illustrations are from my own photographs taken in the year 1896.

It gives me great pleasure to acknowledge my indebtedness to a large number of reviewers who have shown no less enthusiasm than my own in their endeavours to arouse general interest in the subject of this work. To me the service done is one of great encouragement; for I have only praise to acknowledge.

HENRY W. CAVE.

NUWARA ELIYA,
MARCH, 1900.

MAP OF
CEYLON.
PALKS STRAIT
GULF OF MANNAR
NORTHERN PROVINCE
NORTH CENTRAL PROVINCE
NORTH WESTERN PROVINCE
PROVINCE OF UVA
SOUTHERN PROVINCE
SABARAGAMUWA
INDIAN OCEAN
BAY OF BENGAL
Anuradhapura
Jaffna
Mannar
Trincomalie
Batticaloa
Badulla
Kandy
Colombo
Galle

CONTENTS.

PAGE

CHAPTER I.

THE GOLDEN AGE OF LANKA - - - - 1—12

CHAPTER II.

THE JOURNEY TO ANURADHAPURA - - - 13—31

CHAPTER III.

MIHINTALE: THE CRADLE OF BUDDHISM IN CEYLON - 32—48

CHAPTER IV.

THE CITY OF ANURADHAPURA - - - 49—118

CHAPTER V.

THE ROCK FORTRESS OF SIGIRI - - - - 119—130

CHAPTER VI.

THE LAKE OF MINNERIA - - - - 131—140

CHAPTER VII.

THE CITY OF POLONNARUWA - - - - 141—159

CHAPTER VIII.

THE ROCK TEMPLES OF DAMBULLA AND ALUWIHARI - 160—165

FULL PAGE PLATES.

THE RUINED CITIES OF CEYLON.

I.	Rock Temple at Dambulla . . .	*Frontispiece*	
II.	The Kandyan District . .	*Facing page*	14
III.	Aluwihari	,,	18
IV.	Rest-House at Nalanda . .	,,	20
V.	Kekirawa	,,	26
VI.	Mihintale	,,	32
VII.	Flight of Stairs at Mihintale .	,,	34
VIII.	Maha Seya Dagaba	,,	36
IX.	Remains of Rock Dwellings at Mihintale	,,	46
X.	The Mahamegha Garden in 1896	,,	48
XI.	Thuparama Dagaba	,,	52
XII.	Monolithic Cistern	,,	54
XIII.	Pandu Orua	,,	56
XIV.	Entrance to the Bo-Tree Enclosure	,,	58
XV.	Isurumuniya Temple	,,	62
XVI.	Sculptured Tablet at Isurumuniya	,,	64
XVII.	Remains of the Brazen Palace .	,,	66
XVIII.	Ruanweli Dagaba	,,	68
XIX.	Ruanweli Dagaba showing the Elephant Wall . . .	,,	70

FULL PAGE PLATES.

XX.	Miniature Dagaba on the Ruanweli Platform	*Facing page*	72
XXI.	Statues of King Dutthagamini and three Buddhas	,,	74
XXII.	Inscription of Nessanka Malla	,,	76
XXIII.	Remains near the Ruanweli Dagaba	,,	86
XXIV.	Pokuna	,,	88
XXV.	Kuttam-Pokuna	,,	90
XXVI.	Abhayagiriya Dagaba	,,	92
XXVII.	East end of Southern Altar of Abhayagiriya Dagaba	,,	92
XXVIII.	West end of Southern Altar of Abhayagiriya Dagaba	,,	92
XXIX.	Carved Stelæ at Abhayagiriya Dagaba	,,	92
XXX.	Remains of the Peacock Palace	,,	94
XXXI.	Jetawanarama Dagaba at Anuradhapura	,,	96
XXXII.	Moonstone and Steps	,,	98
XXXIII.	Termination of Coping at Maha Sen's Palace	,,	98
XXXIV.	Remains of Pavilion *(Third Century)*	,,	100
XXXV.	Moonstone, Guardstone and Steps	,,	102
XXXVI.	Relic Receptacle	,,	104
XXXVII.	Stone Canopy	,,	104
XXXVIII.	Remains in Process of Excavation	,,	106
XXXIX.	Buddhist Railing restored	,,	108
XL.	Monolithic Statue of Buddha	,,	110
XLI.	Galge, or Rock Chamber	,,	112
XLII.	Ruins of the Dalada Maligawa	,,	114
XLIII.	Remains of an Ancient Street	,,	116
XLIV.	Modern Native Dwellings	,,	118
XLV.	Sigiri	,,	120
XLVI.	Remains of the Galleries of Sigiri	,,	124
XLVII.	In the Gallery of Sigiri	,,	124
XLVIII.	Copying the Frescoes of Sigiri	,,	126

FULL PAGE PLATES.

		Facing page	
XLIX.	Excavations on the Summit of Sigiri	,,	128
L.	Minneria	,,	132
LI.	Returning from Polonnaruwa at Eventide	,,	134
LII.	En Route for Polonnaruwa . .	,,	136
LIII.	Elephant Hunters at Polonnaruwa	,,	138
LIV.	Jetawanarama at Polonnaruwa .	,,	140
LV.	Jetawanarama from the North .	,,	142
LVI.	Jetawanarama from the South-West	,,	142
LVII.	Thuparama at Polonnaruwa .	,,	144
LVIII.	Entrance to the Thuparama at Polonnaruwa . . .	,,	146
LIX.	Curious Column and Ruins . .	,,	148
LX.	Kotuwa	,,	150
LXI.	Sat-Mahal-Prasada	,,	152
LXII.	Dalada Maligawa at Polonnaruwa	,,	154
LXIII.	Rock Temple at Polonnaruwa .	,,	156
LXIV.	Statue of King Parakrama . .	,,	158
LXV.	Frescoes at the Aluwihari Rock Temple	,,	164

THE

RUINED CITIES OF CEYLON.

CHAPTER I.

THE GOLDEN AGE OF LANKA.

TO few Europeans in Ceylon is the subject of the present volume more than an empty name, and to the most well informed at home the ruined cities of Anuradhapura and Polonnaruwa have never entered into the region of the actual. If these pages are fortunate enough to arouse some interest in wonders with which only the remains of the ancient civilization of the Valley of the Nile can in any way be compared, the present volume will have received its only justification.

It is somewhat difficult at this day to realise the conditions of existence of the Singhalese more than two thousand years ago, but the attempt must be made, however imperfectly, if we are to understand the remains that we are about to explore. In our task we shall receive guidance and corroboration and the not unneedful correction from the stones themselves that bear their history writ in imperishable symbols confirming the almost contemporary literary sources of our information.

To this end let us take an imaginary glimpse of the island as it was about two centuries after the introduction of Buddhism, and at the condition of those provinces where dense forest now enfolds the remains of mighty cities.

Ceylon was the chief emporium of the eastern world. The merchant fleets of India, China, Persia, and Arabia entered its ports with silks, carpets, cloth of gold, sandalwood, horses, chariots, and slaves. There they met not only to barter with one another, but to traffic with the Singhalese, whose gems were coveted by the nobles and princes of every country. There was no king in India whose wealth could compare with that of the ruler of Ceylon, and the precious products of his dominions readily commanded ample supplies of the luxuries of other nations.

The Singhalese had no need themselves to convey their parcels of pearls, sapphires, and rubies to distant countries. Such wealth brought their wants to their very doors. Wherefore no vessel of their own is visible amongst the motley throng that ride at anchor within the harbours so bountifully provided by nature A few small dhoneys constructed of planks sewn together by threads of coir serve all local requirements, and as yet they have no fleet.

The whole circuit of the coast-line is fringed with stately palms as at the present day, but within this waving belt there is an entire absence of the impenetrable jungles that now cover the land. From north to south the prospect is one of fertility and resource. The forest-capped mountains rise from cultivated valleys whose green crops are watered by artificial lakes that set at nought the periodical droughts to which the Northern provinces are subject. River courses have been deflected to every depression that might serve as a natural receptacle, and the escape of the waters controlled by huge dams and sluices. Elephants tamed to complete obedience are engaged in the construction of the massive stone conduits and channels which convey the streams to the gardens and fields at the will of the husbandman, making the periods of cultivation entirely subservient to his will. We see nothing about these artificial lakes to suggest the prosaic "tanks" by which they are now familiarly known. Such skilful advantage is taken of natural undulations that the beauty of the landscape is enhanced rather than impaired by these works of utility. Each lake is a broad expanse of rippling waters dotted with wooded islands, the haunt of the pelican and flamingo. To its edge sweep down verdant pastures, broken only by groups of limes, jak, breadfruit, and other trees, in whose grateful shade browse herds of spotted deer.

Over a space of ten thousand square miles cultivation asserts uninterrupted sway. Large tracts of rice and garden are seen reaching far away to the horizon, each cluster having its own lakelet fed from the parent tank and thus ensured of a never-failing harvest.

This ideal condition of culture is due to the ingenuity of a people who have risen to the call of necessity and made their land the adequate support of millions; whereas an indolent race, though few in number, must inevitably have starved, as in fact it did when many centuries later the work of irrigation was neglected.

The culture of flowers is such an important industry in every district that it is at once evident there must be an extensive demand for fragrant blossoms. And this is no matter for surprise, as we are in a Buddhist country at a time when the whole nation is assiduous in its observance of a ceremonial in which offerings of flowers play an important part.

We notice also the same care expended on the cultivation of roots, vegetables, and fruits, traceable to the Buddhist injunction against taking animal life. The existence of such a precept is not the least among the marvels of this wonderful land; for the hills which rise from the cultivated plains to the south are peopled with animals of the most dangerous and destructive kind. Herds of elephants trespass upon the surrounding crops;

the wild pig takes his tithes also; the deer inhabiting the groves strays down to the green sward that encircles the lakes, only to become the prey of the leopard that infests every portion of the denser thickets. Even the deadly cobra, guilty of thousands of human lives, is an object of veneration rather than abhorrence, for did he not spread his hood to shield the lord Buddha? *

The order and contentment prevailing amongst the rural population surprise us no less than the perfection of method in the operations of agriculture. These people work to feed not only themselves but also the millions inhabiting the vast cities and occupied, as we shall see, in pursuits that create no wealth, but rather have for their object its dissipation in gorgeous ritual.

It is true that these habits of industry are acquired under a system of forced labour. A life of idleness would not be possible even were it desired. The common folk are required by a despotic monarch to cultivate the land; but the system of raja-kariya, or labour at the king's command, is brought into force only for the construction of their largest works of irrigation. This coercion is, however, the secret of their wealth and happiness, for the habits thus imposed upon them from without render their country healthy and fertile; while their simple home life,

* The legend is that the king of the cobras spread his great hood over Buddha to shade him from the sun while he sat absorbed in profound meditation.

undisturbed by care or ambition, favours the increase of population. Throughout the country great blocks of solid gneiss, sometimes found in the natural formation of a hill-side, sometimes detached by the hand of man, are engraved with injunctions for the maintenance of the system of cultivation and of unity and concord among the people.

In the very centre of this stretch of cultivation lies the mighty city of Anuradhapura. The lofty palaces and monuments of its sacred enclosure tower above the rest of the buildings which cover the land for the space of two hundred and fifty square miles. At all approaches ornamental causeways with massive granite paving converge upon the gates and hint by the rich carvings of their marble curbs at the cunning of the artificer within. The colossal bastions on the walls serve the citizens for the defence of their sacred treasures. Thousands of people are passing to and fro under the avenues of noble tamarinds that shade the broad streets. Crowds of elephants, some with gilded howdahs, with their burden of nobles in silk apparel pass near us. On entering the gates, instead of crowded buildings as in a modern city, we see monastery and temple, palace and shrine, spaced with fine lawns and extensive beds of sweet-smelling flowers, diversified by groups of palms and spice trees.

As we walk along the level highway to the sacred

bo-tree the perfume of jessamine and champac is wafted in the breeze. There is a quiet and reverential bearing amongst the people, and the whole place wears a sacred air. Silent crowds are walking towards the large square enclosure in the middle of the Mahámégha garden, where the leaves of the sacred peepul may be seen quivering above the ornamental stone terraces that surround it. The sanctity with which the tree is regarded can be gathered from the splendour of the structure that invests it, and the care with which it is guarded. An extensive wall of granite, with cornices and coping enamelled with chunam resembling ivory, forms the boundary of a marble-paved court, to which there are four entrances of great architectural merit. Each of these is canopied with a roof of brass supported by twenty pillars, each hewn out of a single stone, set in a raised stylobate of immense granite slabs with bold curbings.*

This is reached by a flight of sculptured steps, the first of which is an exquisitely carved semi-circular slab with a guardian on either side in bas relief. Within the court are lavishly embellished halls containing images of Buddha, some carved in stone and others worked in precious metals. An inner enclosure is formed by tiers of stone terraces raised around the sacred tree, the central object of unceasing veneration as an

* The appearance at the present day may be seen by reference to Plate xiv.

offshoot from the very tree under which Gotama sat until he attained perfection. It is therefore naturally held to be endowed with miraculous power for promoting the spiritual welfare of believers. They crowd the court by day and night. No sooner has the sun gone down than a myriad lamps light up the scene, which is all the more impressive in its contrast with the dark shadows of night beyond.

From the Mahámégha garden, broad streets, spanned by arches hung with gay creepers with their sprays of scarlet, lead to palaces whose golden pinnacles glitter in the sky and to stately shrines on whose white domes the sunbeams glisten with radiant glory. Slender columns of granite with exquisitely carved capitals and festooned with garlands border all the ways. Between the columns stand vessels with blossoms that fill the air with perfume, and statues holding lamps. Thousands of yellow-robed monks pass in stately procession, headed by princes and nobles upon gaily caparisoned elephants; for the national life within the sacred precincts is a perennial drama of ceremonial observances. The chief events of Buddha's life are represented in miracle-plays, and performed in spacious theatres with realistic scenery. Dancing halls are amongst the most popular institutions, and the music of shells and drums resounds in every street.

From the courtyard of the Brazen Palace the

thunder of sixty-four kinds of drums announces that the king, surrounded by a thousand priests, has taken his seat on the ivory throne in the great hall. This hall is the central apartment of the building, around and above which are a thousand rooms disposed in nine stores. The massive structure is built upon eighteen hundred monoliths* covered with chased copper and set with precious stones. Even the lines of the roof are picked out with sparkling gems, and the gorgeous richness of the whole edifice within and without almost passes comprehension. This palace has been bestowed by the king upon the priesthood. It represents the supreme efforts of architect, artist, and builder, and stands without a peer among the many mansions of the holy city.

But even this is dwarfed by the massive shrines that rear their heads in all directions. The new religion has filled its votaries with almost superhuman energy, and only the very hills themselves can compare with the buildings which are the outward expression of their devotion. Foundations, laid to the depth of one hundred feet, are composed of alternate strata of stone and iron cemented one on the other. Upon these pedestals of massive granite are placed and surrounded by sculptured elephants, which appear as bearers of the superstructure, which rises to a height of

*These monoliths stripped of their copper facing may be seen on reference to Plate xvii., facing page 66.

four hundred feet and contains millions of tons of solid masonry. At the four points there are shrines approached by handsome flights of steps; and to these come thousands of worshippers, all of whom grace the altars with gifts of flowers. Not only are the steps and shrines strewn with blossoms, but on days of festival the entire dome is festooned from base to summit with choicest flowers till it resembles a huge bridal bouquet, and over it sprays of water continually play.

There is ample evidence on every hand that religion is not cultivated to the exclusion or even at the expense of cleanliness. The pokuna or bath is quite as ubiquitous as the shrine and monastery, and is constructed on a commensurate scale. There are many measuring about one hundred and fifty by sixty feet, and twenty-five feet in depth, paved with marble, with tiers of granite rising from the floor to the surface. The upper part is adorned with beautiful mouldings, and at either end are flights of marble steps with handsome balustrades.

Here and there are temples hewn out of the solid rock, with chapels for the reception of images of Buddha. All around within and without the solid mass of gneiss is carved with scenes of his life or engraved with precepts of his faith.

Even more worthy of note are the extensive monasteries attached to every temple and shrine, many of them as large as an English country town. Especially beautiful are the designs of the steps leading to the entrance halls. They are supported on either side by gracefully sculptured guardians. The rich scrolls of the balustrading and the intricate carving of the moon-stones to represent a sacred lotus blossom surrounded by semi-circular fillets of horses, bullocks, elephants, and geese in rows, claim a large share of attention.

For a space of twenty square miles extends the inner city, entirely devoted to religious edifices and the palaces of the king and nobles; but beyond this for two hundred and fifty square miles stretch the hives of industry that support it. There are streets without number, each assigned to a particular class of artizans; the potters, blacksmiths, sandal makers, carpenters, stone workers, goldsmiths, tanners, ivory carvers, gilders, and others, are all separately located. The completeness of organization is thorough, and even if the aim is a misdirected one, the results are astounding, and only possible under a unanimous belief in the one religion, to which all industry is subservient. From the rude manufacture of sun-dried bricks to the fashioning of miniature trees with roots of coral, stems of silver, leaves of gold, and flowers of gems, every effort is directed to the service of religion.

A careful investigation of authentic history convinces us that these ancient cities, with their marvellous buildings and splendid resources, were the outcome of the religious enthusiasm which followed the universal reception of Buddhism by the Singhalese nation.

CHAPTER II.

THE JOURNEY TO ANURADHAPURA.

WE have had a glimpse of the golden age of Lanka, and it is now time to set out on our journey and to fill in the sketch that has been drawn by an examination of the ruins themselves, with the help afforded by ancient Singhalese literature.

Only a portion of the journey presents any considerable difficulties to the traveller, but preliminary arrangements of an extensive character are necessary, and a committee of ways and means is indispensable.

The time needed is at least a month from the date of leaving Colombo, which is the starting point for most travellers. From Colombo we journey by rail to Matale, about one hundred miles, reaching the middle of the island and the northernmost limit of European cultivation. The ruined cities of Anuradhapura and Polonnaruwa are situated, the former seventy miles direct north of Matale, and the latter fifty miles to the north-east. In view of the fact that Matale is the most northerly point of the railway, we must there collect our forces and material for the rest of the journey, which will be made over roads, good, bad, and indifferent, and through rugged jungle paths interspersed with swamps, of which nothing can be predicated save their malarial qualities.

We shall find it advisable to requisition a pair of horses and a spring waggon, two bullock-carts to carry provisions, beds, and camp furniture; three pairs of bullocks, one as a reserve in case of lameness or accident to the others; two horse-keepers; three bullock drivers; a cook and cook's mate; and about fifteen coolies. This somewhat formidable array is necessary because many of the places that we intend to visit lie far from the roads that have recently been made through the province, and are only to be reached by jungle tracks of the roughest description.

Anuradhapura, the oldest and by far the most interesting of the ancient cities, is now reached by a pleasant drive direct to the north from Matale, but Sigiri and Polonnaruwa lie far to the east of the main road, and for them about midway between Matale and Anuradhapura we shall branch off into mere jungle tracks. It is convenient therefore to drive on to Anuradhapura and Mihintale, while the jungle party proceeds thirty miles to Dambulla, the starting point for the more troublesome part of the journey.

The carts are laden with tinned and bottled

SCENERY OF THE KANDYAN DISTRICT.

provisions for about twenty days, including about fifty dozen of soda water, for we trust the fluid of the jungle nowhere, even for boiling rice or making tea, and in some places we shall even prefer a few bottles for the purpose of personal ablution. Of all these things the cook is placed in charge, with instructions to await us at Dambulla.

So far we have passed through the unrivalled scenery of the Kandyan district, of which, as it has been described in another volume,* only a glimpse is here given (Plate ii. facing page 14). In this picture will be noticed a curious crag called Ootooankanda, which was in the early sixties the stronghold of a famous Singhalese bandit, who for years terrorised the district, and whose exploits in robbery and murder have already reached the legendary stage.

Although the chief end of our journey is the exploration of the ruined cities, we shall find some incidental enjoyment on the way in observing the quaint manners and methods of the natives, which are so foreign to those of our western civilization. The exciting causes of pleasure and pain, joy or sorrow, flowing from conditions and events so simple and even trivial, constitute a never-failing source of interest, and we cannot but feel some satisfaction in contrasting their condition

---

* The Author's "Picturesque Ceylon," Vol ii.

of only a few years ago, as gleaned from their own lips, with that of to-day.

Not the least deserving of mention for his share in this great amelioration is the late Sir William Gregory, who, with true insight, sought in the golden age of Ceylon the most effectual means of restoring health and plenty to a people decimated by disease and hunger owing to the destruction of the great works of irrigation devised by their wise ancestors.

Twenty-five years ago the people had reached a stage of extreme destitution. By a frightful disease called "parangi," begotten of indifferent food, whole villages were becoming depopulated, and but for the action then taken by the Government they must have soon reached extinction. There were no roads for communication with the more flourishing parts of the country; their ancient tanks which had for centuries been in disrepair were becoming absolutely useless as a safeguard against drought, and the whole population seemed resigned to the inevitable. They even seem to have been unable to protect themselves against the beasts that disputed with them the right to their country, and faces torn and mangled in desperate encounters with bears were so common as to call for no expression of surprise.

The first step towards improving their condition was the construction of the road by which we are about to proceed to Anuradhapura. Then came the question of combating the disease that was everywhere rife among them. For this, Dr. Kynsey, the Government medical adviser, prescribed the simple and effective remedy of pure air and water, to be obtained by making clearings in the forests and jungles and by restoring the ancient tanks. The Government thereupon issued an ordinance providing for the cost of the masonry of the sluices on condition that the inhabitants themselves repaired the earth-works. The villagers, encouraged by the interest displayed on their behalf, applied themselves bravely to the task, with the further result that the work of improvement has not stood still, and now the number of tanks in working order may be reckoned by the hundred. Round many of the villages, too, the forest has been cleared; and in place of impenetrable jungle stand beautiful parks which provide a fit setting for the stately ruins that repose in their midst. In every locality thus treated the health of the inhabitants has greatly improved, and in place of the fever-stricken district of a quarter of a century ago, there is a large tract which, for beauty and antiquarian interest, is, I do not hesitate to write, without a rival, and which, if not yet perfectly salubrious, is already safe for the ordinary traveller throughout its most interesting parts.

Before we leave Matale it will repay us to walk leisurely through the town, which contains one of the largest purely native bazaars in Ceylon extending for almost a mile in one long street shaded by a fine avenue of rain trees, so called from the circumstance that at night the leaves fold into a kind of sack in which the moisture condenses, and at sunrise when the leaves open is discharged in quite a shower. Here are to be seen the necessaries and luxuries for the supply of the native community throughout the large and important planting district of which Matale is the centre. All the shops are after the fashion of open stalls, and the traders, their goods and transactions, from one end of the street to the other, are open to the gaze of the passers by. The barber, the tinker, the merchant of gay coloured cloths, and the curry-stuff vendor, are all doing a roaring trade. The mellifluous tones of Ramasamy's voice are unceasing, and the stranger will not fail to be struck with surprise at the inordinate amount of talking required by every trifling bargain.

But Matale is not without its antiquarian interest also. Before we have proceeded a mile on our journey, a path on the left of the road, which might easily escape notice, leads to a famous cave of both archæological and literary interest—the Cave-Temple of Aluwihari (Plate iii). At present we pass on, reserving it for our return, when we shall be in possession of information that will add to our interest and heighten our

ALUWIHARE.

appreciation. And for the same reason we shall resist every temptation to turn aside till we reach Mihintale, the cradle of Buddhism in Ceylon. The country which we pass through for the first stage is grandly undulated, and for the most part under cultivation of rice, cocoa, and tea. The roadside scenes have the characteristics of the Kandyan district, and are especially beautiful in their wealth and variety of tropical foliage. We halt here and there to examine some method of native agriculture, or to inspect some indigenous manufacture.

Our attention is arrested by a clay-bedaubed wheel lying near the threshold of a palm-thatched hut. The native potter perceiving our interest sets it going, while a bright-eyed urchin, clothed only in the dark brown tints of his shiny skin, hastens forward with a handful of clay, which in the twinkling of an eye the potter converts into an earthenware chattie or water-urn. Again he casts a lump upon the spinning wheel and with surprising dexterity a shapely bowl is fashioned. We question him on his output, his earnings, the daily round of his life, his ambitions—which we find have no existence—and then proceed to discover whether he enjoys real contentment. Finding that he is possessed of this priceless blessing, we decide that this wayside potter with his earnings of fivepence a day has the advantage of his fellow-craftsman of

Sèvres or Worcester with his higher wages and greater needs.

The next diversion is caused by a gang of some fifty or sixty coolies—men, women, and children—approaching from the north, each with a little bundle containing the household gods and entire possessions of its bearer; and as they halt with curious eyes directed towards us, we stop to enquire whence they come and whither they go. We find they are on the march from Southern India, attracted by the fourpence a day obtainable in the planting districts of Ceylon, as compared with the penny that represented their full earning capacity in their own country.

At the fourteenth mile we reach the small but picturesque village of Nalande. We make for the rest-house, near the entrance of which there is a good specimen of the sacred bo-tree with monkeys gambolling in its branches. This is our first introduction to one of the principal objects of veneration of all Buddhists. The rest-house which we have chosen to illustrate as a specimen of the picturesque and comfortable little hostelries erected by the Government at easy stages on this road for the use of travellers is, as may be seen by reference to our illustration, built in park-like grounds and embowered in remarkably fine tamarind trees. It is neatly furnished and altogether so comfortable that we begin to feel astonished at the comparative luxury and ease of

REST-HOUSE AT NALANDA.

travelling on this part of our journey. We bait our horses and remain here to lunch, after which we stroll out to make the acquaintance of the villagers.

There are only a few native huts scattered here and there in the jungle, but already we notice indications of the poverty and sickness which still to some extent characterise the province. Children are lying on the mud floors of the little thatched sheds instead of merrily skipping about the roads as in the villages that we have passed through, and anxious mothers are nursing listless and fretful infants, sure signs of the presence of malaria. We are travelling in January, when the rainy season has scarcely ended, and swamps of saturated and decaying vegetation abound in all uncleared and uncultivated regions. Still the country is far more picturesque than later in the year, when the raging torrents of the rivers are reduced to feeble rills, and the beds of dilapidated tanks are dry; for this reason we choose January, although extra precautions are necessary in the shape of frequent doses of quinine and the avoidance of night exposure.

We have now left behind the cultivated lands of the Kandyan province and proceed through dense forest for the rest of the journey. Habitations become less frequent during the next stage of twenty miles which brings us to Dambulla. Here we find another excellent rest-house and take up our quarters for the night. It is the half-way halting place between Matale and Anuradhapura, and, being much used, is placed in charge of an experienced attendant who keeps it well provisioned. He is one of the smartest of his class, and surprises us no less by his facility and intelligence in the dual capacity of cook and valet than by his ingenuity in other matters. Being aware that in these rest-houses the most palatable dish that can be procured is curry and rice, we inform him that we want plenty of this and nothing else for our dinner. But such a request is incomprehensible to him. He has never heard of an Englishman dining from a single course, and judging by his experience he considers variety to be quite as essential as plenty. But though his larder is not remarkable for the diversity of its contents, he sets to work with the following menu as the surprising result:—Chicken soup á la mulligatawny—chicken cutlets—roast fowl—grilled chicken—chicken curry—anchovy eggs. Six courses of chicken, disguised and otherwise! Well, we shall go further and fare worse before we reach Colombo.

After dinner we find amusement in the visitors' book. This is not a mere autograph album, but a book in which visitors record their impressions of the general merits of the house from the traveller's point of view. It is inspected periodically by the road committee under whose control these caravanserais are. For the most part it is filled with testimony to the deserts of the custodian, often framed in amusing phraseology but intended to express complete satisfaction. However, at length a visitor arrives in a hypercritical mood and destroys the unison with the following remarks:—

"Rest-house requires white and colour washing, also painting. Back verandah and pillars filthy from dirty hands and chunam marks. Rest-house keeper never thinks of cleaning brass door handles or doors. Two dead frogs have been stuck on dining-room door since Friday, and he never saw it until he was shown. The rest-house keeper has a godown and room of his own, and should not be allowed to dine with his son-in-law in the back verandah; the smell of their food is far from pleasant to those who occupy the rest-house. Lazy coolies, squalling baby and podians,* also women, are very much 'in evidence'; baby especially so at night. Rubbish, such as cocoanut leaves, stable straw sweepings, tins, paper, &c., should be burnt, and not left in a heap in the compound close to rest-house."

The ingenuity displayed in the following note appended by the rest-house keeper is delicious:—

"I beg respectfully to explain first that the doors are always cleaned in the morning when there are no gentlemen at the rest-house. The gentleman arrived here on Friday, and as he was rising late, I did not clean the doors as usual,

* Native Children.

fearing that the banging of the doors will annoy him. Scores of frogs (gasgembas) are weekly destroyed, and it is not strange that one may get crushed between the door post, especially as a fear to disturb gentlemen of a nervous temperament, who are late risers, makes me do the cleaning as noiselessly as possible.

"When gentlemen come to the rest-house with their servants they often order me to feed them, which I do in the back verandah when visitors are in the rest-house; not knowing when we will be wanted, I and servants take our hurried meal in the back verandah, but if there is wrong I will discontinue the practice.

"The 'coolies and podians, also women,' complained of by the gentleman, are old friends and relations of the few coolies who were laying gravel on the approaches.

"Every morning just at daylight the compounds are swept of all the straw, pieces of paper, &c. (mostly thrown by the servants of gentlemen visitors), but the heavy blowing always sends rubbish of this sort to the compound, and as sweeping once in every hour is not practicable, they often lie about.

"The rest-house, though it has a clean compound all round, is yet surrounded by dwelling-houses, and I cannot prevent babies of these very prolific parents from crying in the night. It is true I am adopting a baby, but being well cared for he is noiseless, especially at night.

"I regret very much to have to state that during all the time every visitor, including H. E. the Governor, has pleased at the manner this establishment is kept up; the only dissentient is this gentleman.

"JOHANNIS PERERA, Rest-house Keeper."

We enquire of the resourceful and ingenious Johannis who gave him that name, and we find that his ancestors were converted to Catholicism by the Portuguese four centuries ago, and that his family has remained steadfast in the faith ever since. When asked whether he ever feels any inclination towards Buddhism, he replies, suiting his action to his words by drawing his hand across his throat: "If killing me, I not give up my religion." We find that religion with him is more than a pious opinion; the noisy baby complained of is a poor little foundling that he discovered deserted in the jungle. He tends it with the greatest care, sitting up through the night endeavouring to soothe its quivering limbs, and yet carries on his duties during the day with marvellous energy; and we have nothing but praise for him, both as rest-house keeper and as man.

The village consists of a double row of mud huts which do duty as caddies or native shops, and extends for about two hundred yards at the foot of a solitary mass of rock rising from the plain to a height of about five hundred feet and about a mile in circumference. It is smooth, rounded, and ugly, but about half way to the summit there are some cave-temples of considerable interest which we shall visit on our return.

The remaining forty-two miles to Anuradhapura is a somewhat monotonous drive through forest, unrelieved by anything save the myriads of gorgeous birds and the creatures that here and there dart to and fro across the road. By walking on ahead we are enabled to make many an addition to our collection, and we not infrequently bring down a good specimen with a shot from the carriage. The thickets are almost impenetrable, and although we hear noises and movements innumerable—the strident call of the peacock, the hoarse rattle of deer, and the chattering of monkeys—the network of creepers, with which the trees are bound together in a tangled mass, forbids pursuit save where elephants have cleared the way.

The villages of Kekirawa and Tirappanne, at the fourteenth and twenty-eighth miles respectively from Dambulla, form easy stages for rest and refreshment. Both have good rest-houses similar to that at Nalanda. Kekirawa is a very fair specimen of the village that has been improved by clearing away the jungle (see Plate v). Though it is picturesque in itself, it will be noticed that the huts are squalid and lack the surroundings of palms, plantains, and creepers that we should

KEKIRAWA.

see in any other province of Ceylon. Indeed there is nothing but the scantily-clad people and the heat to remind us that we are in the Tropics.

We meet a shooting party here with whom we share the rest-house, which soon becomes a temple of mirth. The attendant here is another entertaining character, not only for his skill in the culinary art, but also for his acquaintance with interesting events of the past and his facility in recounting his own experiences. Noticing his African cast of features, we open conversation with him on the question of his nationality.

"You are not a Singhalese man, rest-house keeper?"

"No, Sar. Kaffir, Sar. I belonged to Ceylon Rifle Regiment."

"Then perhaps you can tell us something about Sardiel, the Singhalese highwayman, who, I believe, was captured by your regiment."

"Yes, Sar. My company was sent to take him in his stronghold. That place, I think calling Ootooankanda. Sergeant Momatam wounded him in the knee. Sardiel then shooting Sergeant Momatam in forehead and killed him. Sardiel's master forsaking him, then shots hitting. Sardiel not doing anything without magic."

"Tell me all you know about him, and what you saw."

"Sar, there are many stories. I went with my company. We fired on Sardiel's hut in the mountain, and he fired on us. We could not kill him because of his master. Honourable Saunders was there. He not wanting any nonsense, and made rush into Sardiel's house and seized him. We bound him to back of carriage and marched to Kandy with him. He was tried and hung. Then English peoples very afraid his master bringing him to life again, and they got twelve European doctors* to see that he was dead. Then putting him into iron box and locking and making iron chains round and putting deep in the ground and covering over with cement."

"But do you believe what you are saying?"

"Sar, (with great indignation) it is quite true. Sardiel never doing anything without his master."

"Then why did they not capture his master?"

"Sar, he was magician."

"If you believe this how do you account for Mr. Saunders taking him?"

"Sar, his master saying: 'Your time is come. You have stolen many guns and money, and murdered many peoples, now I give you up,' and then Sardiel was powerless."

Noticing that one of our party is amused above the rest by the Kaffir's remarks, we find, by a curious coincidence, that he can supply the authentic details of the story, since he himself was one of the jury that tried the bandit and saw him hanged. Our Plate facing page 14 gives a view of

* The "twelve European doctors" were no doubt the twelve jurymen.

the rugged crag called Ootooankanda, and the beautiful country which was the scene of the exploits of Sardiel, whose authentic history is something like the following:—He was a little insignificant Singhalese, "with nothing in him but the devil," and from his stature one would expect an ordinary boy of fourteen to have proved more than his match. Originally a barrack boy in Colombo, detected in theft, he fled and adopted robbery as a profession. He appears to have gathered around him some kindred spirits, and to have fixed on Ootooankanda, in the district of Keigalle as his home. He was dreaded by Europeans and natives alike, showing marvellous resource in stealing arms and ammunition and using them with deadly effect in his nefarious enterprises. After he had so terrorised the district that no contractor would undertake the transit of goods from Colombo to Kandy without an escort, a reward of £100 was offered for his apprehension. The police were powerless against him. He shot six of them on a single occasion, and a pathetic story is told of one of these ill-fated constables. He had previously been censured by his superiors for his failure to capture Sardiel, and when on this occasion he was determined on retrieving his character, his father who accompanied, seeing him shot down, ran forward exclaiming: "You have killed my son, kill me also," was instantly shot down, and died within a few hours. Other attempts were made by the police to capture him, but without result. At length he was taken by Mr. F.R. (now Sir Frederick) Saunders, then district judge of Keigalle, with a company of the Ceylon Rifles, as our Kaffir friend describes, and with him the only survivor of his band to whom the Kaffir had in true Oriental fashion attributed miraculous powers. There was immense excitement over the trial and execution of the two miscreants, but the Kaffir's story of the precautions after the scoundrels were hanged, needless to say, can only be attributed to the effect of such excitement on popular imagination.

All this serves to while away the time necessary to bait our horses and ourselves; but it may here be mentioned that Kekirawa is a convenient place as head-quarters for a visit to the great tank of Kalawewa, five miles distant by jungle path or seven miles by road. This gigantic reservoir of about six thousand acres is a good locality for sport, and as it abounds in archæological interest, and is in addition very picturesque, it will well repay a second visit.

We now push on to the wonderful city. As we approach, greater variety of colour is noticeable in the foliage; open park-like scenery takes the place of dense forest, and we are particularly attracted by the beauty of the trees, especially the ebony, the satinwood, the halmilla, with its large cabbage-like leaves, pretty cassias, the great kumbuk, which lines the banks of the river with its buttress-like stems, the wood apple, which favours the swampy ground, and the fig in all its varieties. The climbing plants are no less striking, and their fantastic forms are wonderful and bewildering. The golden crowns of climbing lilies, the brilliant convolvuli, the mosses and lichens and the multitude of ferns, with thousands of beautiful plants whose identity is only known to the accomplished botanist, adorn the walks and drives that have been formed amidst the mouldering fragments of the ancient city. We are made aware of our arrival at the sacred precincts by the immense number of stone pillars which stand in groups on every cleared space, and here we rest for the night.

CHAPTER III.

MIHINTALE.

THE history of the ruined cities of Ceylon is intimately connected with the religion of Buddha, and the building of the monuments which we are about to survey was directly due to the adoption of that cult by the Singhalese nation in the third century before Christ. With the prior condition of the country we shall concern ourselves only so far as to enquire who or of what race were the Singhalese, and what were the circumstances that led to their unanimous reception of a new creed with such fervour as is evidenced by the remains of their sacred buildings and literature.

Before the dawn of civilization in India, when as yet the Sanskrit speaking Aryans of the north had not emerged from obscurity, the whole country was peopled by half-savage races in various stages of barbarism. Some of these aborigines settled in Ceylon, where a few scattered types even still remain. Shunning every opportunity of contact with other races, they still dwell in the forest, where they live on the products of the chase,

MIHINTALE,

display the most elementary notions of religion in the form of snake and demon worship, and exercise powers of reason very little superior to those of the lower animals with whom they share the rocks and caves of districts otherwise forsaken. They are referred to in the ancient literature of the country with much contempt as Yakkas, or barbarians. Their conquerors seem to have forced them to slave labour on the tanks constructed in very early times, but there is no reference to them after the third century A.D., and it may be inferred from this and the exclusive and barbarous condition of the small remnants of the tribe that they became entirely cut off from the Singhalese after a short period of subjection.

A few categorical statements regarding the origin of the Singhalese race will serve our purpose better than the introduction of debateable matter and the myths of the early chronicles. The Singhalese were Aryan settlers from North-Central India, and their language was closely affiliated to Pali, a dialect of the Sanskrit which was cultivated by the Aryan invaders of Central India. They settled in Ceylon some centuries before the Buddhist conversion. We know little of their history at this early period; for although the ancient chroniclers professed acquaintance with the minutest details relating to their arrival and settlement in the island, the accounts given are purely mythical. The Mahawansa, a native chronicle that gives many valuable and interesting accounts of later times, indulges in the most extravagant fairy tales in dealing with the national history anterior to the third century B.C. It begins with the story of the arrival of Wijayo, a Singhalese prince, who with his followers is made the hero of adventures so similar to those of Ulysses and Circe in the Odyssey that the chronicler has by some been supposed to have been acquainted with the Homeric poems.

Fortunately, however, we arrive on firmer ground early enough for our purpose of tracing the history of the ancient cities, and all that we need to notice of times prior to their foundation is the simple fact that the Singhalese were in possession of the country, much of which they had brought under cultivation, aided by works of irrigation, an art which they appear to have acquired in prehistoric times. It is safe, moreover, to assume that for some centuries before the arrival of Mahinda, who brought them tidings of the new religion about the year B.C. 307, they had developed resources which were soon to be employed in the building of those great cities, the remains of which we have discovered two thousand years later, and which will take their place among the greatest wonders of the world.

Lastly, it may be safely asserted that the national religion previous to the introduction of Buddhism was Brahman.

FLIGHT OF STAIRS AT MIHINTALE.

It is, however, a great thing that the period of the erection of the buildings whose remains now stand before us falls within the domain of authentic history. Not a single building or sculptured stone has been found that does not come within this period, and it is remarkable that in India no relic of ancient architecture has been discovered of a date anterior to that of the ruined cities of Ceylon, while the history of the latter is infinitely clearer and more reliable than that of the adjoining continent, a circumstance due to the careful preservation by the Singhalese of the olas on which the events of very early times were inscribed.

Mihintale first claims our attention because here began the Buddhist influence, the efficient cause of all the constructive energy which the Singhalese displayed in the erection of their vast cities and monuments. Eight miles to the east of the sacred part of the city of Anuradhapura the rocky mountain, now called Mihintale, rises abruptly from the plain to the height of a thousand feet. Its slopes are now covered with dense forest from the base almost to the summit, with the exception of the space occupied by a grand stairway of granite slabs which lead from the level plain to the highest peak. These steps, one thousand eight hundred and forty in number, render easy an ascent which must have been originally very toilsome. They are laid on the eastern side which is the least steep, the southern face being almost precipitous. Our illustrations (Plates vi and vii facing pages 32 and 34) depict one of the lower and the topmost flights. The last hundred and fifty steps, as seen in Plate vi, are hewn in the solid rock, and at the top is visible the north-east side of the ruined Etwehera dagaba.

At first sight this picture conveys only the impression of a natural hill with precipitous sides covered with vegetation, and were not curiosity aroused by the flight of steps and the robed monk descending, the dagaba might easily escape notice. A closer examination, however, reveals the fact that it is not a natural hill, but a gigantic ruined edifice, in the erection of which many millions of bricks were brought to the top of the mountain and carefully laid. Near it there are other dagabas of great size One, called the Maha Seya (see Plate facing page 36) is placed in a position whence grand views of the surrounding country are obtained. The summit of this can be reached by the adventurous climber, and the exertion, if not the danger, is well repaid by the striking spectacle of the ruined shrines of Anuradhapura rising above a sea of foliage, and the glistening waters of the ancient artificial lakes relieving the immense stretches of forest. For twenty centuries this mass of brickwork defied the destructive tooth of time, and the disintegrating forces of vegetable growth; but a few years ago it showed signs of

MAHA SEYA DAGABA.

collapse on the west face, and underwent some repairs by the Ceylon Government. Our illustration presents a near view from the south, showing the portion cleared of vegetation and repaired. Some idea of the proportion of this dagaba may be gathered by noticing that what appears to be grass upon the upper portion of the structure is in reality a mass of forest trees that have grown up from seeds dropped by birds.

There are many other interesting remains on this mountain sacred to the memory of Mahinda, the royal apostle of Buddha in Ceylon, but before we proceed to them some account of Mahinda and his mission, as recorded in the ancient writings, may be of interest. This account is, of course, to a great extent coloured by imagination, and the facts embellished in true Oriental fashion, but the story may be accepted in its main features. It may not be assumed with safety that every one who takes up this volume is acquainted with the early history of Buddhism, and consequently the story of Mahinda must be prefaced by a brief account of the origin of the cult which he introduced, and of the circumstances which led to its adoption in Ceylon.

In the sixth century, B.C., the Aryans already inhabited the valley of the Ganges, and were divided into various tribes, one of the least of which was that of the Sakyans, who dwelt some hundred miles north-east of Benares. Of this race was Gotama, the founder of Buddhism, his father being chief of the clan, which possessed an influence out of all proportion to its number. Gotama very early chose the life of a mendicant, left his home, and went on foot to Benares, to teach the principles of his philosophy. His method appealed to the Indian mind, and he soon obtained numerous followers. His doctrines were accepted with enthusiasm, probably because they were found to be better suited to the needs of the people of the time than those hitherto prevailing.

About two hundred miles east of Benares were the states of Magadha. Thither the fame of Gotama's teaching soon spread, and the king, Bimbisara, repairing to the presence of Gotama, became a convert. This royal patronage soon led to the wide popularity of the religion of the Sakyan philosopher, and multitudes including the most revered ascetics of the kingdom, adopted its tenets.

We have not much reason to discuss here the principles of Buddhism as introduced by Gotama, except for the purpose of arriving at the origin of the influence which led to the building of the sacred cities. It will, however, be useful to note briefly the main features of the system, which presupposes the doctrine of transmigration.

A buddha is a being who has passed through countless lives and has in each successive re-birth added something to his merits, by which he ultimately becomes endowed with supernatural powers. Upon attaining buddhahood, which is the supreme phase of existence, the buddha is enabled to direct all beings to the path that leads to final extinction. At his death he ceases to exist; but his precepts are regarded as laws of religion. Buddhas appear only at intervals of time inconceivably vast. The broad outline of the Buddha's teaching is contained in the four dogmas –

(1) Existence is sorrow;

(2) Desire for existence is the cause of sorrow;

(3) The cessation of sorrow is effected by the eradication of desire;

(4) The way of living which leads to the extinction of sorrow is the practice of right faith, right resolve, right speech, right action, right living, right effort, right recollectedness, and right meditation, according to the example of the Buddha.

The effect of entirely eliminating desire is final extinction. Unless existence is dissolved by the total destruction of desire re-birth takes place, thus perpetuating sorrow; and, in proportion as Buddhist precepts have been observed or disregarded, so is the re-birth favourable or otherwise. The wicked suffer retribution by unfavourable transmigration, and all beings good or bad pass through an endless succession of lives unless freed from existence by the attainment of a clear insight into the causes of sorrow and the practice of the life that sets them free.

These were the doctrines introduced by the Buddha in the sixth century B.C. However they may be regarded to-day, they were undoubtedly superior to those of Brahmanism, and their ready adoption by millions of people shows how suited they were to the Indian mind.

At the time of Gotama's death, about B.C. 477, the Magadhan state was one of small prestige, but during the two centuries that followed it became a powerful empire, with the march of which the Sakyan's teaching kept time. The brotherhoods formed by his followers during his lifetime practised the course of life that he taught, and thus by example and tradition the system spread and descended from one generation to another.

The great teacher left no writings to guide his adherents, but soon after his death his teachings were collected under the authority of Councils of the Community, and to these were added the records of all his words and deeds that could be garnered for the instruction and example of posterity.

In the early part of the third century B.C. the Greeks invaded India, an event of no small importance to the future of Buddhism. The Magadhan state received the support of the invaders, with the result that it soon became a mighty empire embracing nearly the whole of India; and the ruler of this vast domain, Asoka, was an earnest patron of Buddhism. He was originally a Brahman, but upon his conversion he became a very zealot for the new faith, sending missionaries to many countries, and amongst them his son, Prince Mahinda, who was sent to Ceylon, the field of labour to which his training was especially directed.

The Singhalese, as we have already said, were of the same race as the Magadhans, and it is reasonable to suppose that they spoke the same language. Moreover, the monarchs of the two countries were on terms of friendship. Tissa, the Singhalese king, who had upon coming to the throne succeeded to very great wealth, despatched ambassadors to his friend Asoka with costly presents. That monarch, in acknowledging the treasures, sent many valuable gifts to Tissa in return, accompanied by the following exhortation:—"I have taken refuge in Buddha, his religion, and his priesthood; I have avowed myself a devotee in the religion of the descendant of Sakya. Ruler of men, imbuing thy mind with the conviction of the truth of these supreme blessings, with unfeigned faith do thou also take refuge in this salvation."

Upon this Mahinda proceeded to Ceylon to follow the above message with personal appeals

His meeting with the king at Mihintale is described in the Mahawansa with a wealth of picturesque incident in which a sprinkling of signs and wonders authenticates the importance of his mission. The portion which bears the test of reason, and which from contemporary evidence may in substance be accepted, tells of Mahinda's arrival upon the mountain of Mihintale, accompanied by a few monks. Here they met the king out hunting with a large retinue, and Mahinda thus addressed his majesty: "We are the ministers and disciples of the Lord of the true faith: in compassion for thee, Maharajah, we have repaired hither." The king, recollecting the message of his friend Asoka, was convinced that they were ministers of the faith. Laying aside his bow and arrow he conversed graciously with them. Seeing the other members of the mission, he enquired "Whence come these?" "With me," replied Mahinda. Then the king asked if there were any other priests like unto them, to which Mahinda replied: "Jambudipa itself glitters with yellow robes; there are disciples of Buddha, who have fully acquired the three sanctifications, who are perfect masters of the knowledge which procures bliss, the saints who have the gift of prophecy and divination, are numerous." For the purpose of ascertaining the capacity of the king, Mahinda interrogated him; and as he propounded question after question the monarch solved them satisfactorily. "What is this tree called?" asked Mahinda. "A mango," replied the king. "Besides this are there any other mango trees?" "There are many." "Besides this mango and those other mangoes, are there any other trees in the world?" "Yes, there are many others, but they are not mangoes." "Besides the other mango trees and the trees that are not mangoes, is there any other?" "Yes, this mango." "Ruler of men," cried Mahinda, "thou art wise." The king having thus been proved capable of understanding, a discourse on Buddhist doctrine was delivered, and he and his train were then and there converted.

King Tissa rejoices exceedingly to find that Mahinda is the son of his friend the emperor, and invites him to the capital. Then follows the conversion of the queen and her attendants and the reception of Buddhism by the whole nation.

The Buddha is said to have visited Ceylon on several occasions, but we have no very convincing evidence of this. The accounts given in the ancient chronicles were written too long after his death, and have too much of a miraculous element to be regarded as of any historical value, but as they are accepted by the Buddhists as part of their religious belief some reference to them may be expected. The Buddha first prepares the way for Mahinda by clearing the island of the local demons or yakkas. The Mahawansa says that it was known by the Buddha that Lanka (Ceylon) would be the place where his religion would be most glorified, and that it was needful that the yakkas by whom it was inhabited should be removed. Knowing the spot where he would find the yakkas assembled, he proceeded thither by an aërial route, and hovering above them struck terror into their host by storm, tempest, and darkness. The yakkas, overwhelmed with awe, supplicated to be released from their terror. He replied "I will release you, but give unto me here by unanimous consent a place for me to alight on." The yakkas replied that they would bestow on him the whole country. He then descended, and spreading his carpet upon the ground sat down upon it, causing the fringe of the carpet to blaze with flames of fire, which extended on all sides until the terrified yakkas were driven to the very shores of the island. As they stood there he caused the delightful island of Giri to approach the coast, when they gladly rushed upon it to escape the conflagration. The island with new inhabitants then drifted to its former position. The demons having been thus satisfactorily disposed of, Buddha folded up his carpet, and the Dévas—a higher order of supernatural beings—assembled. These he converted in large numbers, and amongst them Sumana, the Déva of the mountain now known as Adam's Peak. To him he gave a handful of his hyacinthine locks, which the Déva enshrined in a golden casket, and covering this with an emerald dome, preserved it as an object of veneration for future ages.

The aborigines are frequently referred to at this period as Nagas, or snake-worshippers, and it is recorded that Buddha on his second visit converted the Naga king. A few years later he revisited his royal convert, who entertained him and his attendant disciples at Kelani, near Colombo, providing them with a celestial banquet. It was on this occasion that Buddha rose aloft in the air and left the impression of his foot upon the mountain of Sumana (Adam's Peak.) If his object was to sanctify for ever the Peak, he certainly succeeded, for now, in this nineteenth century, two thousand five hundred years after the event, the annual stream of pilgrims who at the risk of their lives climb the precipitous sides of the mountain to salute the sacred footprint is ever on the increase.

On a higher plane of historical truth lies Mahinda's visit to Mihintale, which is attested by contemporary evidence.

Having now some knowledge of the causes which led to the veneration of the sacred localities and the foundation of their buildings, we must resume our inspection of the remains at Mihintale. King Tissa's conversion was commemorated by a great vihara or monastery erected on the very spot, and by the construction of a large number of monastic dwellings in the rock, the remains of which are amongst the most interesting features of the mountain at this day. After the completion and establishment of the monastery, the building of the grand stairway was begun, and continued for generations by pious pilgrims. Meanwhile many a shrine was added by successive monarchs to the memory of the great Mahinda till the mountain was literally covered with sacred buildings. In the solid granite of the steeper slopes were engraved the instructions for the priests, dealing with every detail of their life and every item of ceremonial observance.

These inscriptions, which are still legible, tell us that none who destroyed life in any way were permitted to live near the mountain; special offices were allotted to various servants and workmen; accounts were to be strictly kept and examined at an assembly of priests; certain allowances of money to every person engaged in the temple service were made for the purchase of flowers, so that none might appear without an offering; cells are assigned to the readers, expounders, and preachers; hours of rising, of meditation, and of ablution are prescribed; careful attention to food and diet for the sick is enjoined; there are instructions to servants of every

REMAINS OF ROCK DWELLINGS AT MIHINTALE.

kind, warders, receivers of revenue, clerks, watchmen, physicians, surgeons, laundrymen, and others, the minuteness of detail giving an excellent idea of the completeness of arrangement for the orderly and beautiful keeping of the venerated locality.

Amongst other interesting remains on the mountain is the Naga Pokuna or snake bathing pool. This is hewn out of the solid rock, and is one hundred and thirty feet in length and of extremely picturesque appearance. On the rock which overhangs one side of the pool is an immense five-hooded cobra carved in high relief. Having regard to the role of protector assigned to the cobra in the ancient legend already referred to, this monster, with his hood spreading fully six feet across, doubtless possessed prophylactic virtues, which were assisted by the ceremonial ablutions for which this weird and mysterious looking bath was constructed.

Amongst the best preserved relics is the Ambustele Dagaba which enshrines the ashes of Mahinda, who ended his days on the spot where his successful mission began. The shrine marks, it is said, the very piece of ground where the first meeting of the monarch Tissa and the royal missionary took place. It is built of stone instead of the usual brick, and is surrounded by fifty slender octagonal pillars with sculptured capitals.

Near the dagaba is a narrow ledge high up

the side of a precipitous rock known as Mahinda's bed. Though there is nothing at first sight to suggest repose it may well be credited that to this lonely spot the apostle was wont to retreat to renew in the contemplation of the vista spread out beneath him that spiritual fire which may have been burning low after a prolonged contact with the world. Certainly the view is one of majestic grandeur. For some hundreds of feet ledge after ledge supports huge fallen boulders of granite, while the forest below extends to the sea in an expanse unbroken save by a few patches of rice which pleasantly relieve the monotony and add colour to the landscape.

THE MAHAMEGHA GARDEN IN 1896.

CHAPTER IV.

ANURADHAPURA.

UPON our return to Anuradhapura we naturally wish first to see the remains of those buildings which were erected by Tissa as a result of his conversion. These we find in that part of the city which was at the time of Mahinda's visit the Mahamegha, or king's pleasure garden. The tradition is that the report of Bimbisara, king of Magadha, having presented his own pleasure garden to Buddha and of its being accepted by him for the use of the priests had reached the ears of Tissa, and in imitation of this pious example he dedicated the Mahamegha to sacred purposes. This garden of twenty square miles in extent was in the centre of the royal city, eight miles to the west of Mihintale. The gift was important, as signifying the royal protection extended to the new religion, and like all matters of special interest it received much attention from the ancient chronicler, as may be seen by the following extract from the Mahawansa :—

"In the morning, notice having been previously given by beat of drums, the celebrated capital, the road to the thera's (chief priest's) residence, and the residence itself on all sides, having been decorated, the lord of chariots, decked in all the insignia of royalty, seated in his chariot, attended by his ministers and the women of the palace, and escorted by the martial array of his realm, repaired to the temple constructed by himself, accompanied by this great procession.

"There, having approached the theras worthy of veneration and bowed down to them, proceeding together with the theras to the upper ferry of the river, he made his progress, ploughing the ground with a golden plough to mark the limits for the consecration. The superb state elephants, Mahapaduma and Kunjara were harnessed to the golden plough. Beginning at the first Kuntamalaka, this monarch, sole ruler of the people, accompanied by the theras, and attended by the four constituent hosts of his military array, himself held the haft of the plough.

"Surrounded by exquisitely painted vases, carried in procession, and gorgeous flags; trays containing sandal dust; mirrors with gold and silver handles; baskets borne down by the weight of flowers; triumphal arches made of plantain trees, and females holding up umbrellas and other decorations; excited by the symphony of every kind of music; encompassed by the martial might of his empire; overwhelmed by the shouts of gratitude and festivity which welcomed him from the four quarters of the earth;—this lord of the land made his progress, ploughing and exhibiting furrows, amidst enthusiastic acclamations, hundreds of waving handkerchiefs, and the exultations produced by the presentation of superb offerings.

"The eminent saint, the Mahathera, distinctly fixed the points defining the boundary, as marked by the furrows made by the king's plough. Having fixed the position for the erection of thirty-two sacred edifices, as well as the Thuparama Dagaba, and having according to the forms already observed, defined the inner boundaries thereof, this sanctified person on that same day completed the definition of all the boundary lines. At the completion of the junction of the sacred boundary line the earth quaked."

Having thus dedicated the royal precincts of the city to religious purposes, Tissa's next object was to hallow them by the presence of a relic of the Buddha himself.

Here again we plunge into myth of the highest order to obtain a grain or two of actual fact. We accept as authentic the statement that the Thuparama was the first of the large shrines built upon this sacred ground, and that it was erected by King Tissa. It is quite likely, too, that he endeavoured to procure a true relic of the Buddha, and that he sent to his friend the

Emperor Asoka to obtain one; but a simple recital of such a proceeding would be quite unworthy of the oldest shrine in Ceylon; and so Tissa is said to have had recourse to supernatural means to obtain the needful relic, and to have asked the gods themselves for the right collar bone of the Buddha. A nephew of Mahinda was chosen for the mission, and instructed to address the Emperor Asoka as follows: "Maharajah, thine ally Tissa, now converted to the faith of Buddha, is anxious to build a dagaba. Thou possessest many corporeal relics of the Muni; bestow some of those relics, and the dish used at his meals by the divine teacher." He was next to proceed to Sakka, the chief of the Dévas, and thus addressing him: "King of Dévas, thou possessest the right canine tooth relic, as well as the right collar bone relic, of the deity worthily worshipped by the three worlds: continue to worship that tooth relic, but bestow the collar bone of the divine teacher. Lord of Dévas! demur not in matters involving the salvation of the land of Lanka." The relic was surrendered by the gods and conveyed to Anuradhapura, where it performed many miracles before it reached the receptacle in the Thuparama. Its concluding feat was to rise from the back of the elephant that conveyed it to the shrine to the height of five hundred cubits, and thence display itself to the astonished populace,

THUPARAMA DAGABA.

whose hair stood on end at the sight of flames of fire and streams of water issuing from it.

But it is not within our present purpose to quote all the legends that embellish the history contained in the ancient Singhalese writings, and we must pass on to the shrine itself, built by Tissa about the year B.C. 307.

This monument is in itself evidence of the remarkable skill of architect, builder, and sculptor in Ceylon at a period anterior to that of any existing monument on the mainland. The upper portion of the structure has been renovated by the devotees of modern times, but the carvings and other work of the lower portion remain untouched. A great deal of excavation is, however, still necessary to expose the platform at the base.* All the Ceylon dagabas are of this bell shape, but their circumference varies from a few feet to over eleven hundred, some of them containing enough masonry to build a town for twenty-five thousand inhabitants. The Thuparama is small compared with many of them, the diameter of the bell being about forty feet and its height about sixty.

The portion of the basement immediately beneath the bell is undoubtedly ancient. It consists of two stages; the lower, about three and a half feet high, is faced with dressed stone

* This excavation was completed in 1896, shortly after the publication of the first edition of this work.

and belted with bold mouldings; the upper retires a couple of feet, and upon that is a terrace six feet wide running right round the dagaba. The whole of the interior is believed to be solid brick. Below the basement of the bell all has more or less been buried in earth and débris, the accumulation of ages; some excavation has, however, disclosed a circular platform of about one hundred and sixty feet in diameter, raised to about twelve feet above the original level of the ground. The base of this platform, which is reached by two flights of stone steps, is also of brick and is ornamented with bold mouldings to a height of about five feet, and above this the wall is surrounded with semi-octagonal pilasters.

The most attractive feature of the dagaba, however, is the arrangement of ornamental pillars on the platform. A large number, as may be seen by a glance at our illustration, facing page 52, are still erect. They are all slender monoliths of elegant proportions. The carvings of the capitals are singularly beautiful; they contain folial ornaments as well as grotesque figure-sculptures, and are fringed to a depth of more than a foot with tassels depending from the mouths of curious masks. These pillars are placed in four concentric circles, and decrease in height as the circles expand, the innermost being twenty-three feet and those of the outside circle fourteen feet high.

MONOLITHIC CISTERN.

There has been a great deal of speculation as to the possible structural use of these pillars. Some have suggested that they supported a roof which extended over the entire dagaba, others that they were erected in order to carry pictures representing scenes of Buddhist history, hung from beams supported on their capitals. It is very likely that they served some purpose besides that of mere ornament, but what that was we are hardly likely now to discover, as no allusion is made to them in any of the ancient chronicles. I am inclined to think that they were surmounted by emblematic figures, and were intended primarily as ornaments in themselves. They were doubtless used on festal occasions to suspend strings of lamps and garlands, always one of the chief features of Buddhist ceremonial.

Of the original one hundred and seventy-six pillars only thirty-one remain now standing entire with their capitals. There was probably a walled enclosure to the dagaba, and it has been suggested that upon this wall a conical roof was raised over the whole structure partially supported by the pillars. I cannot, however, find any reason to adopt this theory.

Near the Thuparama there is a remarkably fine trough carved out of a single block of granite. Its size may be estimated from the old Singhalese woman who stands near it. She volunteered the statement that she was upwards of eighty years of age and that she was in charge of the shrine. The trough is undoubtedly very ancient, but its use is a matter of conjecture, some suggesting that it was a receptacle for rice given to the priests.

In the vicinity lies another curious vessel, about seven feet long, also hewn out of a single block. Its chief points are a circular basin and a raised slab, and it is supposed to have been used for dyeing the robes of the priests, being known as a "pandu orua," or dyeing vat. The robes were placed in the basin of yellow dye, and were afterwards spread upon the slab and wrung out with wooden rollers.

The interesting ruins of the Daladá Máligáwa, or Palace of the Tooth, are within the original outer wall of the Thuparama enclosure. This palace was built for the reception of Buddha's tooth upon its arrival in Ceylon in A.D. 311, but we will postpone our remarks upon this until we have visited the ruins of a still older date.

We pass now to another relic which has perhaps attracted more attention than any other—the sacred bo-tree. The royal convert, King Tissa, having succeeded in obtaining a branch of the fig-tree under which the Buddha had been wont to sit in meditation, planted it at Anuradhapura and it is now the venerable tree which we see still flourishing after more than twenty centuries.

PANDU ORUA.

Its offspring have formed a grove which overshadows the ruins of the once beautiful court and the tiers of sculptured terraces which were built around it. All that is left of the magnificent entrance to the enclosure is seen in our picture—a few bare monoliths and the two janitors still at their post.

The story of this tree is intimately connected with that of Mahinda, and therefore goes back to the foundation of Anuradhapura. We have already noticed that the conversion of the people followed immediately upon that of their king, and in the desire to embrace the doctrines of the great preacher the women were not behind, and thousands of them wished to take vows and enter upon a life of asceticism. But Mahinda declared that although they might be converted by his preaching they could take vows only at the hands of a dignitary of their own sex. This difficulty was overcome by sending for his sister Sanghamitta, who had become the prioress of a Buddhist nunnery at Pataliputra. Thither King Tissa's minister, Arittha, was deputed to proceed and invite her to Ceylon for the purpose of initiating the women of the island; and at the same time he was directed to request the Emperor Asoka to allow her to bring with her a branch of the sacred bo-tree under which the Buddha attained perfection. This plan was duly carried into effect; the princess came, and with her the branch from which grew the very tree which still flourishes at Anuradhapura.

Glancing at the story of the Mahawansa, we shall find no exception to the typical manner in which the native historians embellished their descriptions of important events, disguising every fact with a mantle of extravagant romance.

When it was decided that a branch of the original bo-tree should be sent, superhuman aid was immediately forthcoming for the construction of a golden vase for its transit. This vase was moulded to a circumference of fourteen feet and a thickness of eight inches. Then the monarch causing that vase, resplendent like the meridian sun, to be brought, attended by the four constituent hosts of his military array, and by the great body of the priesthood, repaired to the great bo-tree, which was decorated with every variety of ornament, glittering with the variegated splendour of gems, decked with rows of streaming banners, and laden with offerings of flowers of every hue. . . Having bowed down with uplifted hands at eight places, and placed that precious vase on a golden stool, studded with various gems, of such a height that the branch could easily be reached, he ascended it himself for the purpose of obtaining the topmost branch. Using vermilion in a golden pencil, and streaking the branch therewith, he made this solemn declaration and invocation:—"If this right top-

ENTRANCE TO THE BO-TREE ENCLOSURE.

most branch from this bo-tree is destined to depart hence to the land of Lanka, and if my faith in the religion of Buddha be unshaken, let it, self-severed, instantly transplant itself into this golden vase."

The bo-branch, severing itself at the place where the streak was made, rested on the top of the vase, which was filled with scented oil . . . The sovereign on witnessing this miracle, with uplifted hands, while yet standing on the golden stool, set up a shout, which was echoed by the surrounding spectators. The delighted priesthood expressed their joy by shouts of "sahdu," and the crowding multitude, waving thousands of cloths over their heads, cheered . . . The instant the great bo-branch was planted in the vase, the earth quaked, and numerous miracles were manifested. By the din of the separately heard sound of various musical instruments—by the "sahdus" shouted, as well by Dévas and men of the human world as by the host of Dévas and Brahmas of the heavens—by the howling of the elements, the roar of animals, the screeches of birds, and the yells of the yakkas as well as other fierce spirits, together with the crashing concussions of the earthquake, they constituted one universal chaotic uproar.

The vase was then embarked on board a vessel in charge of a large number of royal personages, and accompanied by the monarch was taken down the Ganges to the sea, where the Maharajah disembarked and "stood on the shore with uplifted hands; and gazing on the departing branch, shed tears in the bitterness of his grief. In the agony of parting, the disconsolate Asoka, weeping and lamenting in loud sobs, departed for his own capital."

After a miraculous passage the vessel arrived off the coast of Ceylon and was discerned by the king, who was watching for it from a magnificent hall which had been erected on the shore for the purpose. Upon seeing its approach he exclaimed: "This is the branch from the bo-tree at which Buddha attained Buddhahood," and rushing into the waves up to his neck, he caused the great branch to be lifted up collectively by sixteen castes of persons, and deposited it in the lordly hall on the beach.

It was then placed on a superb car and accompanied by the king was taken along a road sprinkled with white sand and decorated with banners and garlands of flowers to the city of Anuradhapura, which was reached on the fourteenth day. At the hour when shadows are most extended the procession entered the Mahamegha garden, and there the king himself assisted to deposit the vase. In an instant the branch extricated itself, and springing eighty cubits into the air, self-poised and resplendent, it cast forth a halo of rays of six colours. These enchanting rays illuminating the land ascended to the Brahma heavens and continued visible till the sun had sunk into the sea.

Afterwards, the branch descending under the constellation "Rohini," re-entered the vase on the ground, and the earth thereupon quaked. Its roots, rising up out of the mouth of the vase and shooting downwards, descended, forcing it down into the earth. The whole assembled populace made flower and other offerings to the rooted branch. A heavy deluge of rain fell around, and dense cold clouds completely enveloped it in their snowy shrouds. At the end of the seventh day the clouds dispersed and displayed the bo-tree with its halo. . . . . . .

This bo-tree, monarch of the forest, endowed with many miraculous powers, has stood for ages in the delightful Mahamegha garden in Lanka, promoting the spiritual welfare of the inhabitants and the propagation of the true religion.*

There is good reason to accept the main facts of the above story, notwithstanding the fairy tale into which they have been woven. The subsequent history of the venerable tree has been less poetically chronicled, and details with great exactness the functions held in its honour, together with reliable information on matters connected with its careful preservation and the adoration

* This account is condensed from Mr. Turnour's translation of the early part of the Mahawansa, written in the fifth century.

bestowed upon it. That it escaped destruction by the enemies of Buddhism throughout many invasions is perhaps attributable to the fact that the same species is held in veneration by the Hindoos who, while destroying its surrounding monuments, would have spared the tree itself.

Another very ancient and interesting foundation attributed to King Tissa is the Isurumuniya Temple. This curious building, carved out of the natural rock, occupies a romantic position. Before and behind lie large lotus ponds on whose banks huge crocodiles may occasionally be seen. We may easily photograph them from a distance by means of a telescope lens, but they object to be taken at any shorter range. We may approach them with a hand camera, but immediately it is presented to them they dart into the water at lightning speed. These ponds are surrounded by woodland scenery which presents many an artistic feature; but we must be content with a near view of the temple itself. To the right of the entrance will be noticed a large pokuna or bath. This has been restored and is quite fit for its original purpose of ceremonial ablution, but the monks now resident have placed it at the disposal of the crocodiles whom they encourage by providing them with food.

The modern entrance to the shrine, with its tiled roof, is in shocking contrast to the rock-building, and unfortunately this is the case with all the ancient rock-temples of the island.

ISURUMUNIYA TEMPLE.

The terraces which lead to the shrine are interesting for their remarkable frescoes and sculptures in bas relief. There are more than twenty of these in the walls, and all of them are exceedingly grotesque. Several are in the form of tablets like the specimen here shown, facing page 64.

In addition to the tablets, the natural rock was frescoed in high relief, and although many of the figures have become hardly discernible owing to the action of the climate during so many centuries, others are still clearly defined and may be seen in our illustration with the aid of a convex lens. Above the corner of the bath are the heads of four elephants, and above them is a sitting figure holding a horse. Similarly there are quaint carvings in many other parts. The doorway is magnificent, and for beautiful carving almost equals anything to be found in Ceylon. There is nothing of special interest about the shrine. It has a figure of Buddha carved out of the solid rock, but the rest of it has been decorated quite recently, and like the entrance porch seems out of harmony with the rest of the place.

The temple is unique in many respects and worthy of a thorough exploration. It was discovered about thirty years ago entirely hidden by jungle, and, of course, in a worse state than at present.

There are doubtless many more remains of this period lying buried in the jungles of Anuradhapura awaiting discovery, but the next we shall tarry to investigate is the Brazen Palace, a building of somewhat later date—the end of the second century B.C.

In the interval between Tissa's death and the building of the Brazen Palace by Dutthagamini, a large number of monasteries were erected and the community of monks greatly increased. But even so early as this after the foundation of the sacred city trouble came in the form of invasion from Southern India. For some years the Tamils held the upper hand, Elara, one of their princes, usurped the Singhalese throne, and the Buddhist cause was in danger of complete annihilation, when the Singhalese king Dutthagamini, stirred by religious enthusiasm, made a desperate stand and recovered his throne. The story of the final combat is worthy of our notice as showing the character of the man who erected the most wonderful of the Anuradhapura monuments.

It was in B.C. 164 that Dutthagamini, having grown weary of the protracted struggles of his army which for some years he had led with varying fortune against Elara, challenged that prince to single combat. Having given orders that no other person should assail Elara, he mounted his favourite war elephant, Kandula, and advanced to meet his adversary. Elara

SCULPTURED TABLET AT ISURUMUNIYA.

hurled the first spear, which Dutthagamini successfully evaded and at once made his own elephant charge with his tusks the elephant of his opponent. After a desperate struggle Elara and his elephant fell together.

Then followed an act of chivalry on the part of Dutthagamini so remarkable that it has been regarded with admiration for twenty centuries. He caused Elara to be cremated on the spot where he fell, and there built a tomb. He further ordained that the tomb should receive honours, and that no one should pass it without some mark of reverence; and even to this day these injunctions are to some extent regarded, and the tomb is still marked by a huge mound.

With the death of Elara the power of the invaders was broken, and the heroic Dutthagamini by his patriotism and bravery restored to the country those conditions of peace and prosperity under which Tissa had been enabled to inaugurate the religious foundations already referred to. To the further development of these he now applied himself.

The community of monks had enormously increased with the popularity of the new religion, and Dutthagamini made their welfare his chiefest care, erecting the Loha Pasada, known as the Brazen Palace, for their accommodation. This remarkable building rested on sixteen hundred monolithic columns of granite, which are all that now remain; their original decoration has disappeared, and we see only that part of them which has defied both time and a whole series of heretic invaders. The basement or setting of this crowd of hoary relics is buried deep in earth that has been for centuries accumulating over the marble floors of the once resplendent halls, and all that is left to us are these pillars partially entombed, but still standing about twelve feet out of the ground (see Plate facing this page).

The history of this wonderful edifice is fully dealt with in the native chronicles, whose accuracy as to the main features is attested in many ways, and not least by the "world of stone columns" that remain.

The following description is taken from the Mahawansa, and was probably written about the fifth century A.D. from records preserved in the monasteries:—

"This palace was one hundred cubits square and of the same height. In it there were nine stories, and in each of them one hundred apartments. All these apartments were highly finished with silver; and the cornices thereof were embellished with gems. The flower-ornaments thereof were also set with gems, and the tinkling festoons were of gold. In this palace there were a thousand dormitories having windows with ornaments which were bright as eyes.

"The monarch caused a gilt hall to be con-

REMAINS OF THE BRAZEN PALACE.

structed in the middle of the palace. This hall was supported on golden pillars, representing lions and other animals as well as the dévatás, and was ornamented with festoons of pearls all around. Exactly in the middle of this hall, which was adorned with the seven treasures, there was a beautiful and enchanting ivory throne. On one side of this throne there was the emblem of the sun in gold; on another the moon in silver; and on the third the stars in pearls. From the golden corners in various places in the hall, bunches of flowers made of various gems were suspended; and between golden creepers there were representations of the Játakas. On this most enchanting throne, covered with a cloth of inestimable value, an ivory fan of exquisite beauty was placed. On the footstool of the throne a pair of slippers ornamented with beads, and above the throne glittered the white canopy of dominion mounted with a silver handle.

"The king caused the palace to be provided suitably with couches and chairs of great value; and in like manner with carpets of woollen fabric; even the laver and its ladle for washing the hands and feet of the priests kept at the door of the temple were made of gold. Who shall describe the other articles used in that palace? The building was covered with brazen tiles; hence it acquired the name of the 'Brazen Palace.'"

The palace did not long remain as originally constructed by Dutthagamini. In the reign of Sadhatissa, about B.C. 140, the number of stories was reduced to seven; and again, about two centuries later, to five. Its history has been marked by many vicissitudes, generally involving the destruction of some of its upper stories. These attacks on the wonderful edifice were not always due to the iconoclastic zeal of Brahman invaders, but to a serious division in the ranks of the Buddhists themselves. About the year B.C. 90 a question arose as to the authority of certain doctrines which one party wished to be included in the canon. The proposal was regarded as an innovation and strenuously opposed by the orthodox fraternity, with the result that those who adhered to the innovation formed themselves into a rival body known as the Abhayagiriya. Hence the great Brazen Palace, which had originally been the residence of the highest ascetics, was dependent for its preservation on the varying fortunes of its orthodox inhabitants. This division, which marred the unity of Buddhism in Ceylon for fourteen centuries, was perhaps at the height of its bitterness when Maha Sen came to the throne at the beginning of the third century. He adopted the heresy above referred to and pulled down the Brazen Palace in order to enrich the rival monastery with its treasures. This apostate king, however,

RUANWELI DAGABA.

afterwards recanted, and in his penitence he restored the palace once more to its ancient splendour, and rebuilt all the other monasteries that he had destroyed.

From the nature of its construction as well as the intrinsic value of its decorative materials, the Brazen Palace has always been more exposed to spoliation than the shrines and other buildings whose colossal proportions astonish us as we wander through the sacred city.

A more enduring and not less remarkable piece of work of Dutthagamini has come down to us. The new religion had filled its votaries with almost superhuman energy, and only the very hills themselves could compare with the buildings which were the outward expression of their devotion. Foundations were laid to the depth of one hundred feet and composed of layers of crystallised stone and plates of iron and copper alternately placed and cemented; and upon such basements were piled millions of tons of masonry.

We see the remains of one of these stupendous edifices in the Ruanweli or gold-dust dagaba. Its present appearance from a distance, from which our picture is taken, is that of a conical shaped hill of nearly two hundred feet high, covered with trees and surmounted by a tiny spire. It is, however, a mass of solid brickwork (see Plates facing pages 68 and 70).

Time and the frequent attacks of enemies have

to a great extent obliterated the original design, but there is sufficient of the structure still remaining to verify the accounts of the ancient writers who have transmitted to us full details of the building as it was erected in the second century B.C. We should not readily believe these accounts without the evidence of the ruins. It is as well, therefore, to see what remains before we glance at the first written story of the dagaba.

The ruins of the eastern portico in the foreground of the picture at once suggest an entrance of stately proportions. The pillars are arranged in six parallel rows so that wooden beams might be laid upon them longitudinally and transversely for the support of the ornamental open roof which was undoubtedly there. The boldly sculptured lions of the left front give a clue to the style of ornament adopted.

Upon traversing the passage, which we notice is sufficiently large to admit elephants, we arrive at an extensive court or platform nearly one hundred feet wide and extending round the whole dagaba. This is the path used for processions in which a large number of elephants frequently took part. From this rises another immense square platform measuring about five hundred feet each way and made to appear as if supported by about four hundred elephants. These elephants form the retaining wall; they

RUANWELI DAGABA,

SHOWING THE ELEPHANT PLATFORM PARTIALLY EXCAVATED.

were modelled in brickwork and placed less than two feet apart; only their heads and fore legs appear; their height is about nine feet. Although all that have been excavated are in a terribly dilapidated condition (see Plate facing page 70), there are still evidences here and there of the original treatment and finish. We learn from the native records that they were all coated with a hard and durable white enamel called chunam, and that each had ivory tusks. In protected places portions of the original surface still remain, and the holes in the jaws where the tusks were inserted are still visible.

There are also traces of ornamental trappings which were executed in bold relief; they differ considerably on each elephant, suggesting very great ingenuity on the part of the modellers.

These two platforms form the foundation constructed to sustain the ponderous mass of the solid brick shrine which was built upon it to the height of two hundred and seventy feet, with an equal diameter at the base of the dome.

The upper platform from which the dagaba rises covers an area of about five acres, and is paved with stone slabs; these share the general ruin, due more to ruthless destruction than the ravages of time. We notice that repairs have been effected by fragments of stone taken from other fine buildings; for there are doorsteps, altar slabs, carved stones, of all shapes and sizes, some incised with very quaint devices of evident antiquity, and even huge monoliths from the thresholds of other buildings have been dragged hither to supply the destroyed portions of the original paving.

The objects of interest surrounding the dagaba are very numerous. There are four ornamental altars, and various parts belonging to them scattered everywhere: carved panels, pedestals, scrolls, capitals, friezes, stone tables, elephants' heads, great statues of Buddhas and kings—all these have been excavated within the last twenty-five years.

Our illustration facing page 70 shows how formidable is the business of excavation. The platforms had been buried to the depth shown by the heaps of earth that still surround them and hide the greater portion of the elephant wall.

The same features are observable in the illustration which faces this page. Here upon the platform we notice in its original position a miniature dagaba, of which there were probably many placed around the great shrine as votive offerings. This specimen with the platform below it is composed of a weighty monolith, and does not appear to have been disturbed.

In the far distance is a statue with a pillar of stone at the back of it. This is said to be a statue in dolomite of King Batiyatissa I., who came to the throne B.C. 19. It is eight feet

MINIATURE DAGABA ON THE RUANWELI PLATFORM.

high, much weather worn, and full of fractures.

Near it are four other statues placed with their backs to the dagaba (see Plate facing page 74), three of them representing Buddhas, and the fourth King Dutthagamini. They originally stood in the recesses of a building on the platform, and were dug out during the excavations. They are all sculptured in dolomite; the folds of the priestly robes with their sharp and shallow flutings are very beautifully executed. They were probably once embellished with jewels, the pupils of the eyes consisting of precious stones, and the whole figures being coloured in exact imitation of life.

The figure on the extreme left is said to be that of the king, who is wonderfully preserved considering his great antiquity. The statue is ten feet high, and must have looked very imposing in its original state, the jewelled collars being gilt, and their pearls and gems coloured and polished; even now the features wear a pleasant expression.

The hall where these figures were unearthed was probably built specially for their reception. It is close to their present position, and its threshold is marked by a plain moonstone.

Within a few yards of the statues stands a very fine slab engraved in old Singhalese characters (see Plate facing page 76). This seems to have formed part of the wall at the side of the porch of the hall, and it is still erect between two of the original pillars, being very firmly fixed in a bed of brickwork. The engraved face would thus have been inside the portico. Its date is the latter part of the twelfth century, and it gives some account of various good deeds of the King Kirti Nissanka, who was famous for his attention to the repair and maintenance of religious edifices. After reciting that he "decorated the city like a city of the gods," it ends with an appeal to future princes to protect and preserve the viharas, the people, and the religion.

To give a complete description of the Ruanweli dagaba and of the numerous ruined halls, altars and monuments that form part of or are connected with it would fill a volume at least as large as the present. We must, however, remark briefly on a few more points of special interest.

The three terraces or pasadas round the base of the bell are about seven feet wide, and were used as ambulatories by the worshippers. The uppermost terrace is ornamented with fore-quarters of kneeling elephants to the number of about one hundred and fifty. These are placed on the outer edge at regular intervals all round the dagaba. From the terraces the great hemispherical mass of brickwork was carried to the height of two hundred and seventy feet, including the tee or small spire. Its present appearance,

STATUES OF KING DUTTHAGAMINI AND THREE BUDDHAS.

as may be seen in our Plate facing page 68, is a shapeless mound covered with trees sprung from stray seeds; but beneath those trees are the millions of bricks which were carefully and religiously laid two thousand years ago.

The lower part of the bell has been restored to some extent by pious pilgrims who have from time to time expended considerable sums of money upon it; but the race that could make these immense shrines what they once were has vanished, and with it the conditions which rendered such works possible.

The principal ornaments of the dagaba were the chapels or altars at the four cardinal points. All these are in a very ruinous condition, portions of the friezes carved in quaint designs being strewn about, as also are railings, mouldings, brackets, vases, and sculptures of various kinds. One of these structures, however, has been restored as far as possible from the fragments found lying about at the time of its excavation. There are traces here and there of enamel and colour, especially upon the figure subjects, and it is supposed from this that the whole surface of the altars was covered with that wonderfully durable white enamel called chunam, and that they were made attractive to the native eye by gaudy colouring of the figures and cornices.

In addition to the interesting architectural features of the shrine there are numerous inscriptions in old Singhalese characters, relating to grants of land and other matters connected with the dagaba. The ancient writings refer to a number of monastic edifices that surround it. Of these there are traces; but, since we find even lofty platforms buried in earth and overgrown with grass and trees, the exploration of smaller buildings is easily understood to be a difficult matter. How extensive they must have been we can imagine from the fact that many thousands of monks were attached to the monasteries of each of the large dagabas; and for their personal accommodation, not to speak of the requirements of their religious ceremonies, a vast range of buildings must have been necessary.

Having now glanced at the present condition of the ruined shrine of Ruanweli, we will now turn to the Mahawansa for some particulars of its origin. The chronicler, naturally enough, attributes to a deity the supply of the necessary materials; but the account of the construction is reasonable, and is in many particulars borne out by what we see at the present day. To support a solid mass of masonry two hundred and seventy feet high and nearly a thousand in circumference needed foundations of an extraordinary character, and the attention devoted to this unseen part of the work was justified by results. Its success is evidenced by the fact that not even now has any part of the foundation

INSCRIPTION OF NESSANKA MALLA.

shown the slightest sign of subsidence.

After the necessary excavation had been made, "The monarch Dutthagamini," says the chronicle, "who could discriminate the advantages and disadvantages of things, causing round stones to be brought by means of his soldiers, had them well beaten down with pounders, and to ensure greater durability to the foundation he caused that layer of stones to be trampled by enormous elephants, whose feet were protected by leathern shoes. He had clay spread upon the layer of stones, and upon this he laid bricks; over them a coat of cement; over that a layer of stones; over them a network of iron; over that a layer of phalika stone, and over that he laid a course of common stones. Above the layer of common stones he laid a plate of brass, eight inches thick, embedded in a cement made of the gum of the kappitha tree, diluted in the water of the small red cocoanut. Over that the lord of the chariots laid a plate of silver seven inches thick, cemented in vermilion paint mixed in tila oil.

"The monarch, in his zealous devotion to the cause of religion, having made these preparatory arrangements at the spot where the Mahathupa was to be built, thus addressed the priesthood: 'Revered lords! initiating the construction of the great cétiya, I shall to-morrow lay the festival-brick of the edifice: let all our priesthood assemble there. Let all my pious subjects, provided with offerings, bringing fragrant flowers and other oblations, repair to-morrow to the sight of the Mahathupa."

"The ruler of the land, ever mindful of the welfare of the people, for their accommodation provided at the four gates of the city numerous bath-attendants, barbers, and dressers, as well as clothing, garlands, and savoury provisions. The inhabitants of the capital as well as of the provinces repaired to the thupa.

"The lord of the land, guarded by his officers of state decked in all the insignia of their gala dress, himself captivating all by the splendour of his royal equipment, surrounded by a throng of dancing and singing women—rivalling in beauty the celestial virgins—decorated in their various embellishments, attended by forty thousand men, accompanied by a full band of musicians, repaired to the site, as if he had himself been the king of the Dévas."

Next, the chronicler with evident exaggeration describes the throngs of priests who attended the ceremony from various Indian monasteries. After running up their number to nearly a million, he seems to come to the limit of his notation, and omits his estimate of the full number of Ceylon monks. The account then continues: "These priests, leaving a space in the centre for the king, encircling the site of the cétiya, in due order stood around. The king, having entered the space and seeing the priesthood who had thus arranged themselves, bowed down to them with profound obeisance; and overjoyed at the spectacle, making offerings of fragrant garlands and walking twice round, he stationed himself in the centre on the spot where the filled chalice was placed with all honours. This monarch supremely compassionate, and regardful equally of the welfare of all beings, delighting in the task assigned to him, caused a minister of noble descent, well attired, to hold the end of a fine rod of silver that was fitted into a golden pivot, and began to make him walk round therewith on the prepared ground, with the intent to describe a great circle to mark the base of the cétiya. Thereupon a thera of great spiritual discernment, by name Siddhattha, who had an insight into the future, dissuaded the king, saying to himself, 'the king is about to build a great thupa indeed; so great that while yet it is incomplete he would die: moreover, if the thupa be a very great one it would be exceedingly difficult to keep in repair.' For these reasons, looking into futurity, he prohibited it being constructed of that magnitude. The king, although anxious to build it of that size, by the advice of the priesthood and at the suggestion of the theras, adopting the proposal of the thera Siddhattha, described a circle of more moderate dimensions. The indefatigable monarch placed in the centre eight golden and eight silver vases, and surrounded them with one thousand and eight fresh vases and with cloth in quantities of one hundred and eight pieces. He then caused eight excellent bricks to be placed separately, one in each of the eight quarters, and causing a minister, who was selected and fully arrayed for the purpose, to take up one that was marked with divers signs of prosperity, he laid the first auspicious stone in the fine cement on the eastern quarter; and lo! when jessamine flowers were offered thereunto, the earth quaked."

When the pediment was complete the very important part of constructing the relic chamber was proceeded with. This was placed in the centre and afterwards covered by the mighty mass of brickwork that forms the dagaba.

The Mahawansa gives the following minute description of the formation of the receptacle and the articles placed in it prior to the installation of the relics:—

Six beautiful cloud-coloured stones were procured, in length and breadth eighty cubits and eight inches thick. One of these slabs was placed upon the flower-offering ledge from which the dome was to rise, and four were placed on the four sides in the shape of a box, the remaining one being placed aside to be afterwards used as the cover. "For the centre of this relic receptacle the king caused to be made an exquisitely beautiful bo-tree in precious metals. The height of the stem was eighteen cubits; the root was coral, and was fixed in emerald ground. The stem was of pure silver; its leaves glittered with gems. The faded leaves were of gold; its fruit and tender leaves were of coral. On its stem there were representations of the eight auspicious objects, plants and beautiful rows of quadrupeds and geese. Above this, around the edges of a gorgeous cloth canopy, there was a fringe with a gold border tinkling with pearls, and in various parts garlands of flowers were suspended. At the four corners of the canopy hung bunches composed of pearls, each of them valued at nine lacs. Emblems of the sun, moon, and stars, and the various species of lotuses, represented in gems, were appended to the canopy . . . . At the foot of the bo-tree were arranged rows of vases filled with the various flowers represented in jewellery and with the four kinds of perfumed waters.

"On a golden throne, erected on the eastern side of the bo-tree, the king placed a resplendent golden image of Buddha, in the attitude in which he received buddhahood at the foot of the bo-tree at Uruvela in the kingdom of Magadha. The features and limbs of that image were represented in their several appropriate colours in exquisitely resplendent gems. Near the image of Buddha stood the figure of Mahabrahma bearing the silver canopy of dominion; Sakka, the inaugurator, with his conch; Pancasikha, harp in hand; Kalanga, together with his singers and dancers; the hundred-armed Mara mounted on his elephant and surrounded by his host of attendants." The above was the arrangement of the eastern side. On the other three sides altars were formed in an equally elaborate and costly manner. Groups of figures represented numerous events in the life of Buddha and his various deeds. There was Brahma in the act of supplicating Buddha to expound his doctrines; the advance of King Bimbisara to meet Buddha; the lamentation of Dévas and men on the demise of Buddha, and a large number of other notable occurrences. Flashes of lightning were represented on the cloud-coloured stone walls illuminating and setting off the apartment.

What the relics were that this elaborate receptacle was made to receive is not quite clear, but some were obtained, and for the ceremony of translation a canopy of cloth ornamented with tassels of gems and borders of pearls was arranged above the chamber. On the day of the full moon the monarch enshrined the relics. "He was," says the Mahawansa, "attended by bands of singers and dancers of every description; by his guard of warriors fully caparisoned; by his great military array, consisting of elephants, horses, and chariots, resplendent by the perfection of their equipment; mounting his state carriage, to which four perfectly white steeds of the Sindhava breed were harnessed, he stood under the white canopy of dominion bearing a golden casket for the reception of the relics. Sending forward the superb state elephant, Kandula, fully caparisoned to lead the procession, men and women carrying one thousand and eight exquisitely replenished vases encircled the carriage. Females bearing the same number of baskets of flowers and of torches, and youths in their full dress bearing a thousand and eight superb banners of various colours surrounded the car." Amidst such a scene the monarch Dutthagamini descended into the receptacle carrying the casket of relics on his head and deposited it on the golden altar. He then ordered that the people who desired to do so might place other relics on the top of the shrine of the principal relics before the masonry dome was erected, and thousands availed themselves of the permission.

Now the work of building again proceeded, and the massive dagaba was carried near to completion when King Dutthagamini fell sick. The native chronicle tells a pathetic story of the last scene, describing how the dying monarch was carried to a spot where, in his last moments, he could gaze on his greatest works—the Lohapasada and the Ruanweli Dagaba. Lying on a marble couch which is pointed out to the visitor at the present day, he was comforted by hearing read out an enumeration of his own many pious acts. His favourite priest, who had been a great warrior and had been at his side in twenty-eight battles, was now seated in front of him. The scene is thus referred to in the Mahawansa: "The king thus addressed his favourite priest: 'In times past, supported by thee, one of my warriors, I engaged in battle; now, single-handed, I have commenced my coflict with death. I shall not be allowed to overcome this antagonist.' To this the thera replied: 'Ruler of men, compose thyself. Without subduing sin, the dominion of the foe, the power of the foe, death is invincible. For by our divine teacher it has been announced that all that is launched into this transitory world will most assuredly perish; the whole creation therefore is perishable. The principle of dissolution uninfluenced by the impulses of shame or fear exerts its power, even over Buddha. Hence, impress thyself with the conviction that created things are subject to dissolution, afflicted with griefs, and destitute of immortality. In thy existence immediately preceding the present one, thy ambition to do good was truly great; for when the world of the gods was then even nigh unto thee, and thou couldst have been born therein, thou didst renounce that heavenly beatitude, and repairing thither thou didst perform manifold acts of piety in various ways. Thy object in reducing this realm under one sovereignity was that thou mightest restore the glory of the faith. My Lord, call to thy recollection the many acts of piety performed from that period to the present day, and consolation will be inevitably afforded to thee.' . . . The monarch having derived consolation replied to the thera: 'For four-and-twenty years have I been the patron of the priesthood; may even my corpse be subservient to the protection of the ministers of the faith! Do ye therefore consume the corpse of him who has been as submissive as a slave to the priesthood in some conspicuous spot in the yard of the Uposatha Hall within sight of the Mahathupa.' Having expressed these wishes, he addressed his younger brother: 'My beloved Tissa, do thou complete, in the most efficient and perfect manner all that remains to be done at the Mahathupa; present flower offerings morning and evening; keep up three times a day the sacred service, with full band of musicians. Whatever may have been the offerings prescribed by me to be made to the religion of the deity of happy advent, do thou, my child, keep up without any diminution. My beloved, in no respects in the offices rendered to the priesthood let there be any intermission.' Having thus admonished him, the ruler of the land dropped into silence."

Saddha Tissa carefully carried out the dying wishes of his brother and completed the pinnacle. He also decorated the enclosing wall with elephants, and enamelled the dome with chunam.

Each of several succeeding kings added something to the decoration, and erected more buildings in the precincts of the great shrine. It is recorded of King Batiya Tissa, who reigned between 19 B.C. and 9 A.D., and whose statue near the dagaba we have already noticed, that on one occasion he festooned the dagaba with jessamine from pedestal to pinnacle; and on another he literally buried it in a heap of flowers, which he kept watered by means of machinery constructed for the purpose. Another king is said to have placed a diamond hoop upon the spire.

Whatever percentage we may be inclined to deduct from these accounts, there is no doubt that great wealth was lavished on the structure for many years after its erection. In later times, when the enemies of Buddhism obtained possession of the city, the great dagaba suffered severely; on many occasions it was partially destroyed, and again restored when the power of the Singhalese was temporarily in the ascendant. The last attempt to destroy it is said to have taken place in the thirteenth century.

After our somewhat protracted examination of the Ruanweli, we stroll away from its precincts into one of the open stretches of park-like land

REMAINS NEAR THE RUANWELI DAGABA.

that have been reclaimed from forest and jungle. The gardens that were once an especially beautiful feature of the ancient city were but a few years ago overgrown with trees, and dense thicket had veiled every vestige of brick and stone. Recent clearings have, however, disclosed numberless remains which form a unique feature in the landscape. Clusters of pillars with exquisitely carved capitals, as perfect as if they had recently left the hands of the sculptor, appear interspersed with the groups of trees that have been spared for picturesque effect. Here and there numbers of carved monoliths are lying prostrate, bearing evidence of wilful destruction. As we wander through one of these charming glades we are attracted especially by the group of pillars illustrated in our Plate facing page 86. In almost every instance of such groups the ornamental wings on the landing at the top of the steps are exposed, although the steps and mouldings of the bases are buried in earth. In the illustration here given it will be noticed that these wing-stones, covered with makara and scroll, vie with the carved capitals in their excellent preservation; the fabulous monster forming the upper portion and the lion on the side are still perfect in every particular.

It is probable that these buildings consisted of an entrance hall and a shrine, and that they were purely devoted to religious purposes although they are popularly supposed to have been royal pavilions.

Another very interesting feature of the cleared spaces is the large number of stone-built baths or tanks called "pokunas." There are so many, and they vary so much in architectural treatment, that they must have added greatly to the beautiful aspect of the city. The specimen illustrated in our Plate has been recently restored, and gives a good idea of the original appearance, although much of the ornamental portion is missing. It will be noticed that on one side there is a stone paved terrace, within which is an inner bath. This inner bath was doubtless sheltered by a roof supported upon stone pillars, of which there are several fractured pieces and socket holes remaining. The inner bath leads into a chamber like the opposite one visible in the picture. The walls of these chambers are beautifully-worked single stones, and the tops are covered by enormous slabs of a similar kind, measuring twelve by seven feet.

Wherever clearings are made pokunas are sure to be unearthed. The most interesting example yet discovered is the kuttam-pokuna or twin bath (see Plate facing page 90). This consists of a couple of tanks placed end to end, measuring in all about two hundred and twenty by fifty feet. The left side of the picture serves to show the condition in which the baths were when

POKUNA.

discovered, but on the right we see that some considerable restoration has been effected. The materials are generally found quite complete although dislodged and out of place.

Our photograph was taken in January, before the end of the rainy season, and in consequence the tank appears too full of water to admit of the structure being seen at any considerable depth, and some verbal description is therefore necessary.

The sides are built in projecting tiers of large granite blocks so planned as to form terraces all round the tank at various depths, the maximum depth being about twenty feet. Handsome flights of steps descend to the terraces, some of them having carved scrolls on the wings. The bold mouldings of the parapet give an exceedingly fine effect to the sides. There are signs of rich carvings in many parts of the structure, but every portion is too much defaced to trace the designs.

There is something very weird about these remnants of ancient luxury hidden in the lonely forest. In the dry season of the year, when the ruined terraces of the kuttam-pokuna can be seen to the depth of sixteen feet, this scene is one of the most impressive in Anuradhapura.

We cannot help reflecting, too, that the famous baths of the Roman emperors were constructed contemporaneously with these, and that while those of Caracalla and Diocletian, being built of brick, have crumbled now beyond repair, the picturesque and elegant baths of Dutthagamini with their beautiful terraces and stairways of granite can with little trouble be restored to their pristine condition.

It is impossible to arrive at the exact purpose of the various forms of baths found at Anuradhapura. Some were doubtless attached to the monasteries and used exclusively for ceremonial ablutions; some were private baths of the royal family; others were possibly for public use, and many served as receptacles of the drinking water of the inhabitants. All of them were fed from artificial lakes outside the city.

We have already referred to the usurpation of the throne of Ceylon by the Tamil invader, Elara, and to the combat with Dutthagamini, which resulted in the defeat and death of the usurper. Strange as it may appear, the victor, who had merely regained his birthright, was constrained to make atonement for bloodshed as well as the natural thank offering for his victory, and to this we owe the building of the great monastery of the Brazen Palace and the Ruanweli Dagaba. We find a curious repetition of history in the occurrences that took place about thirty years after his death, when the old enemy again got the upper hand. The king Walagambahu, was deposed, and the usurper, Pulahatta,

KUTTAM-POKUNA.

assumed the sovereignty. Fifteen more years of alien rule ensued, during which no less than four of the usurpers were murdered by their successor, until Walagambahu vanquished the fifth, Dathiya. He then proceeded to raise a monastery and shrine that should eclipse in magnitude those constructed by Dutthagamini under similar circumstances.

The buildings of the monastery have vanished, save only the boundary walls and the stumps of its pillars which are found in large numbers; but the Abhayagiriya Dagaba (Plate facing page 92), of its kind the greatest monument in the world, has defied all the forces of destruction, both of man and nature, and although forsaken for many centuries during which it received its vesture of forest, there is still a very large proportion of the original building left. The native annals give as the measurement of the Abhayagiriya a height of four hundred and five feet, or fifty feet higher than St. Paul's Cathedral, with three hundred and sixty feet as the diameter of the dome. The height is now greatly reduced, but the base covers about eight acres, and sufficiently attests the enormous size of its superstructure. The lower part of the dome is buried under the débris of bricks which must have been hurled from above in infidel attempts at destruction. Beneath this mass the remains of the numerous edifices, altars, and statues, which surrounded the dagaba are for the most part concealed, but excavations at various periods have disclosed some ruins of considerable interest, notably the altars of the four cardinal points, one of which is visible in our illustration facing this page. These altars are very similar to those of the Ruanweli Dagaba but much larger and more elaborate in detail, being about fifty feet in breadth. Many of the carvings are in remarkable preservation considering their vast age and the perils they have experienced. Between the stelæ were the usual strings of carved ornaments, with an additional one composed of running figures representing horses, elephants, bulls, and lions.

The stelæ, of which there are two at each end, are elaborately carved, as will be seen from the accompanying illustrations; the fronts being adorned with a floral decoration springing from a vase, and surmounted by three lions. The return faces are formed of two panels. The upper has a carved male figure (Nâga), with a five-headed cobra as a sort of halo, holding flowers in the right hand and resting the left on his hip. In the lower panel is a female (Nâgani) with single hood; the upper part of whose body is bare, with the exception of some jewellery, while below the waist the limbs are draped in a transparent robe; the ankles are encircled by bangles; and the palm of her right hand supports a vessel, containing a lotus-bud. Adjoining the

ABHAYAGIRIYA DAGABA.

EAST END OF SOUTHERN ALTAR,
ABHAYAGIRIYA DAGABA.

WEST END OF SOUTHERN ALTAR,
ABHAYAGIRIYA DAGABA.

CARVED STELE AT ABHAYAGIRIYA DAGABA.

stelæ is a sculptured seven-headed cobra, the carving of which reproduces the scaly nature of the skin with remarkable fidelity.

The west end of the altar is finished in a similar manner, but here the lower part of the outer stele is destroyed; the upper panel of the return face contains a more elaborately executed male figure, sumptuously attired and bedecked with jewels. There was doubtless the counterpart female figure below, but it has been entirely demolished.

The eastern altar, the first to be excavated, is the most interesting and perfect of all that have yet been discovered.

This dagaba, like the Ruanweli, stands on a square paved platform with sides of about six hundred feet in length, with the usual elephant path below and guard houses at each of the four entrances. Doubtless a very large number of buildings were erected on the platform, but scarcely a vestige of these remains. It will be remembered that Maha Sen enriched the Abhayagiriya with spoils from the Brazen Palace, and it is therefore likely that it was more elaborately embellished than any other dagaba.

Perhaps no ruin at Anuradhapura gives a more complete idea of the utter transience of every perishable part of a building than the so-called Peacock Palace (Plate facing page 94). Not only the superstructure, which was doubtless of woodwork, but every vestige of material other than granite has passed away. This building was erected in the first century of the Christian era, and is said to have owed its title to the brilliance of its external decoration. A circle of finely wrought pillars with beautiful sculptured capitals and the carved wings at the entrance are, as we see, all that remain.

The next group of ruins to which we come belong to the third century, when Maha Sen, on his recantation of his heresy, built another enormous dagaba and a series of smaller religious edifices, of which there are some very interesting remains. This monarch ascended the throne A.D. 275, and died A.D. 302. His support of the schismatics who had seceded from the orthodox faith is attributable to a tutor under whose influence he came by the secret machinations of the party. The result of this was that upon coming to the throne he persecuted those monastic orders that turned a deaf ear to the new doctrines. Hundreds of their buildings were razed to the ground, including the famous Brazen Palace, and the materials were used for the erection of shrines and monasteries for the new sect. When, however, after the lapse of some years, the old faith still held its place in the affections of the people and his throne was endangered by general discontent, he returned to the faith of his fathers, restored all the buildings

REMAINS OF THE PEACOCK PALACE.

that he had destroyed, and reinstated the members of every foundation that he had overthrown.

The inception of the Jetawanarama monastery and dagaba is attributed to the middle period of this monarch's reign in the following quotation from the Mahawansa:—

"The king having had two brazen images or statues cast placed them in the hall of the great bo-tree; and in spite of remonstrance, in his infatuated partiality for the thera Tissa of the Abhayagiriya fraternity—a hypocrite, a dissembler, a companion of sinners, and a vulgar man—constructed the Jetawanarama vihara for him, within the consecrated bounds of the garden called Joti, belonging to the Mahavihara."

The Jetawanarama thus begun before the recantation of the raja was not completed till the reign of his son Kitsiri Maiwan.

We shall merely take a glance at the remains of this great shrine across the glistening waters of the Basawak Kulam from a distance of about two miles (see Plate facing page 96). The Basawak Kulam is one of the lakes constructed as tanks for the supply of water to the city. Although we shall have occasion to refer to these tanks later, we may here notice that this one is said to be the oldest and dates from B.C. 437. The lofty dome which sixteen centuries ago stood gleaming from its ivory-polished surface above the trees and spires which dotted the landscape now stands a desolate mountain of ruined brick-work, over which the forest has crept in pity of its forlorn appearance. Its original height is open to question. It is said to have been three hundred and fifteen feet, but at present it is no more than two hundred and fifty. Like the other dagaba already described it was restored at various periods, and its original outline may have been altered. The spire which still crowns the dome was probably added when the dagaba was restored by king Parakrama Bahu in the eleventh century. Sir Emerson Tennent's pithy remarks upon this monument cannot be overlooked by any writer on Anuradhapura, and must be reproduced here:—

"The solid mass of masonry in this vast mound is prodigious. Its diameter is three hundred and sixty feet, and its present height (including the pedestal and spire) two hundred and forty-nine feet; so that the contents of the semi-circular dome of brickwork and the platform of stone seven hundred and twenty feet square and fifteen feet high exceed twenty millions of cubic feet. Even with the facilities which modern invention supplies for economising labour, the building of such a mass would at present occupy five hundred bricklayers from six to seven years, and would involve an expenditure of at least a million sterling. The materials are sufficient to raise eight thousand houses, each with twenty feet frontage, and these would form thirty streets half a mile in length.

JETAWANARAMA DAGABA AT ANURADHAPURA.

They would construct a town the size of Ipswich or Coventry; they would line an ordinary railway tunnel twenty miles long, or form a wall one foot in thickness and ten feet in height, reaching from London to Edinburgh. Such are the dagabas of Anuradhapura—structures whose stupendous dimensions and the waste and misapplication of labour lavished on them are hardly outdone even in the instance of the Pyramids of Egypt."

All the large dagabas correspond so closely in general design that when you have seen one you may be said to have seen all. Differences exist only in the numerous small structures with which the platforms abound, and in the details of the ornamentation. The Jetawanarama, for instance, has a railing in brickwork, of the form known as a "Buddhist railing"—to which we shall revert hereafter—upon each face of the cube above the dome. The drum sustaining the spire was also the subject of considerable embellishment, and has eight niches in which statues were probably placed. Another peculiarity has been noticed in the shape of the bricks with which the dome was faced. They were very large and wedge-shaped. The measurement of one was found to be—Length, eighteen inches; breadth, twelve inches at one end and nine and a half at the other; thickness, three and a half inches at the broad end and three inches at the other. Some of the panels that decorate the stelæ of the altars have unusual characteristics, particularly one in which a male figure is represented as leading an animal by a rope; and in the panel below a dancing woman attired in transparent clothing. On the paved platforms are lying many enormous slabs and portions of small structures, which show clearly the thoroughness of the destruction carried out by the Tamils. The accumulation of earth around the base of the dome is some thirty feet deep, rendering excavation a somewhat formidable task.

It would be monotonous in the extreme to attempt a description of all the ancient dagabas of Anuradhapura. They are very numerous, and have few points of difference. We now proceed to the interesting ruins said to be the remains of Maha Sen's palace. As they are in close proximity to the great Jetawanarama Dagaba they are probably parts of religious edifices erected by that monarch. There were in all five buildings in one enclosure measuring two hundred feet square. In the centre stood the principal pavilion, the ruins of which are shown in Plate xxxii. At the four corners of the enclosure were the subsidiary edifices, now only traceable by a few stone pillars that mark the site of each. Only so much of the central pavilion as is seen in this Plate has been excavated, but it suffices to show some exquisite carving and to give some idea of the

MOONSTONE AND STEPS.

TERMINATION OF COPING AT MAHA SEN'S PALACE.

importance of the building. The handsome stylobate, although cleared some few years ago, is again covered with jungle. It measures sixty-two by forty-two feet, and had a beautifully moulded base of finely-wrought granite. The superstructure has entirely disappeared. The flight of steps at the entrance needs very few words of description, as it can be seen in our illustration facing page 98. The landing is a fine monolith thirteen feet long and eight wide. On either side of the landing is a grotesque figure. A coping skirts the landing on each side, and terminates in a rectangular block ornamented with a panel containing a seated lion beautifully carved in high relief. This is one of the best pieces of sculpture we shall meet with. The strength of the beast is well brought out, while the uplifted paw and the look of defiance are most suggestive. But as remarkable as the skill of the craftsman is its preservation exposed and uninjured during so many centuries. The steps are ornamented by squatting dwarfs who appear to be supporting the tread; these, too, are well carved; the hands are pressed upon the knees; the waist is girdled, and a jewelled band falls over the shoulders; from the head waving curls are flowing; their ears, arms, elbows, wrists and ankles are adorned with jewelled rings and bangles. The pilasters on either side of each dwarf are carved in similar minute detail and represent bundles of leaves.

At the foot of the steps lies the best preserved moonstone yet discovered. The moonstone, it may be observed, is almost peculiar to Singhalese architecture and is a semi-circular slab forming the doorstep to the principal entrance of a building. Its ornamentation varies considerably as may be seen on comparing Plate with Plate. In our specimen from Maha Sen's pavilion (Plate facing page 98), the innermost fillet contains a floral scroll of lilies; next comes a row of the *hansa*, or sacred goose, each carrying in its beak a lotus-bud with two small leaves; then comes a very handsome scroll of flowers and leaves; after this is a procession of elephants, horses, lions and bulls; and, lastly, a border of rich foliage. All this carving is as sharp and well defined as if it were fresh from the sculptor's chisel, and this in spite of an interval of one thousand six hundred years.

Guard stones and wing stones doubtless formed part of the decoration of these handsome steps, but they have entirely disappeared. The dvarpal stones which face one another on the landing are not so well preserved as the steps, owing to their being exposed while the lower portion of the structure was buried.

Our illustration facing this page represents the remains of one of the so-called pavilions, probably erected in the third century. It has been called the Queen's Pavilion, but was doubt-

REMAINS OF PAVILION (THIRD CENTURY).

less a vihara, or shrine. The most noticeable feature is its massive stylobate of dressed granite ornamented by base mouldings of a very massive character. The pediment is unlike any other that has been discovered, being duplicated and carried higher than usual.

The forest is everywhere teeming with ruins awaiting discovery and excavation. Sometimes the only sign of an important edifice is a single pillar or group of pillars standing above the ground, or perhaps a portion of some stairway which has not yet become entirely hidden by earth. A few years ago Mr. S. M. Burrows discovered the most perfect door-guardians and flight of steps yet unearthed by a very slight indication of the kind referred to. These form the subject of our Illustration facing page 102. I quote Mr. Burrows' own words in reference to them from his Archæological Report:—"On the opposite side of the road to the 'stone canoe,' the extreme tip of what appeared to be a 'dorapáluwa' (door-guardian stone), and some fine pillars at a little distance from it, invited excavation. The result was highly satisfactory. A vihara of the first-class, measuring about eighty feet by sixty, was gradually unearthed, with perhaps the finest flight of stone steps in the ruins. The 'moonstone,' thóugh very large, presents the lotus only, without the usual concentric circles of animal figures; but one at least of the door-guardian stones, standing over five feet high, is unrivalled in excellence of preservation and delicacy of finish. Every detail, both of the central figure and its two attendants, stands out as clear and perfect as when it was first carved; for the stone had fallen head downwards, and was buried under seven or eight feet of earth. On the top of the landing-stone of the stairway are two stone seats hollowed out for the back; and exactly opposite to the stairway on the further side of the vihara is a 'yogi,' or meditation stone, still in position. There is a smaller chapel at each corner of the vihara, approached in like manner by a stone stairway and moonstone. The boundary wall of the vihara presents the usual ogee moulding, carried out in stone near the stairway, and continued in brick."

So called "yogi" stones are very plentiful amongst the ruins of Anuradhapura. They vary very much both in size and the number of square-cut holes they contain. For a long time they were supposed to have been in use by the ancient monks for the purpose of assisting them in their meditation. The method was to sit gazing intently at the holes thinking of nothing until in the entire absence of all distractions the mind could become free from desire and fit to be turned upon self analysis. In this way the monks were supposed to be able to realize their own permanent

MOONSTONE, GUARDSTONES, AND STEPS.

and true nature. A later and more reasonable theory is that these curious stones were receptacles for articles of value deposited as offerings in the shrines, that they were built into the altars, and that the Tamils, aware of their existence, demolished the shrines in search of their precious contents, a proceeding which would more satisfactorily account for their being scattered about.

Among restorations which have recently been carried out is that of a beautiful stone canopy, every piece of which has been found almost perfect. It is very massive, and the moulding is particularly fine. The centre piece alone is said to weigh about five tons. This was another of the discoveries of Mr. Burrows, who gives the following interesting account of his "find" in his report to the Government:—"While superintending some repairs to the so-called 'stone canoe' I was led to explore the forest in the immediate vicinity, and was fortunate enough to discover a magnificent oblong stone with sunk panelled mouldings, which evidently formed the centre-piece of a canopy. It was almost completely buried, face downwards, and consequently was in excellent preservation. The jungle was immediately cleared all round it, and after a diligent search the two flanking stones, which completed the roof, were discovered, together with the stones forming the frieze which ran along the outer edge of the roof. These stones are delicately carved and moulded, and bear altogether six elaborate representations of the familiar 'Buddhist window,' surmounted by a 'makara-torana,' or figure of a mythical beast, the guardian of the entrance. That all these stones formed the roof of a canopy was further proved by the fact that the centre and two flanking stones bore, when first unearthed, plain marks of the squares on to which the sustaining pillars had fitted. Further excavations revealed a platform which exactly corresponded to the measurement of the three roof-stones, an unbroken pillar (together with several fragments of other similar ones) which accurately fitted the square marks still visible on the roof stones, and a staircase of six monolithic steps, each stone bearing traces of an ancient inscription, at right angles to the platform. On communicating these discoveries to His Excellency, the restoration of the canopy was at once ordered. This was a work of several weeks, for we had no appliances at hand for raising heavy stones, except a piece of old chain—(and the three roof-stones together weighed over twenty tons)—and no skilled labour, except a *soi-disant* mason, who had turned his talents to house-breaking, and became a convict in consequence.. From the multitude of pillars in the jungle we selected seven, of precisely the same measurement as the one unbroken pillar discovered, and set up all eight in position. Filling up the whole of

RELIC RECEPTACLE.

STONE CANOPY AT ANURADHAPURA.

the interior with earth to the tops of the pillars, and erecting a sloping platform of earth from the spot where the roof-stones lay to the pillar-tops, we gradually worked the roof-stones upwards, and into position, with crowbars and wooden rollers. The earth between the pillars was then cleared away, and the canopy was complete. It is more than likely that this was the very method by which the building was originally erected nearly two thousand years ago."

The excavations being carried out by the Archæological Commissioner frequently bring to light something of intense interest. One of the best of recent discoveries is the site shown by the Plate facing page 106. For a description of this we cannot do better than consult Mr. H. C. P. Bell's most interesting report, from which the following is quoted:—"Here were found an octagonal shaft and *puhul* capital (a type not hitherto noticed at Anuradhapura) and some narrow moulded slabs deeply morticed. These gave hope of further discovery. When the raised site, six or eight feet above ground level, and some one hundred and forty feet in length by one hundred and ten feet broad, had been cleared of scrub, search was rewarded by a valuable archæological 'find'—a post with three rails attached, in pieces—a genuine fragment of a structural 'Buddhist railing.' Fortunately the peculiar shape of the semi-convex rails had saved them from the fate of the shapely pillars of which but stumps remain in position. The tenons at both ends of the standard explained at once the purpose of the morticed slabs. Here were the rail, post, and plinth; only the coping seemed wanting. After continued search a portion of this was found, showing a few inches above ground, and close to it two slabs of a rounded basement, ten inches in depth, as originally built at right angles to each other. This fixed the south-east corner and determined the plan of the railing which followed the lines of the oblong site. Trial excavation brought up more pieces of rails and coping, and two additional members—a stepped sub-plinth and a low socle below the quarter-round base. There is therefore every reason to hope that by running a trench along the foot of the mound more of this fine railing will be unearthed, and that it may yet be possible to restore it in part to nearly its pristine form.

"The railing consisted of square eight inch standards,—the angle posts probably ten inches by eight inches,—three feet ten inches in height, kept upright by tenons (three inches by two inches) at top and bottom, which fitted mortices in the upper plinth and coping. Three lenticular rails, thirteen and a half inches deep, project from the posts nine inches to twelve inches. The centre rail is separated one and a half inches from the upper and lower rails, and these two inches from coping and plinth respectively. A thin tie (one

REMAINS IN PROCESS OF EXCAVATION.

and a half inch by half inch) strengthens the rails near their lateral extremities. The widest interspaces of the mortice holes on the plinth slabs are but seventeen inches, which would bring the posts within a foot of one another; some would seem to have been still closer together. The coping, rounded at top, is eight inches deep, the upper plinth thirteen inches, and both are delicately moulded.

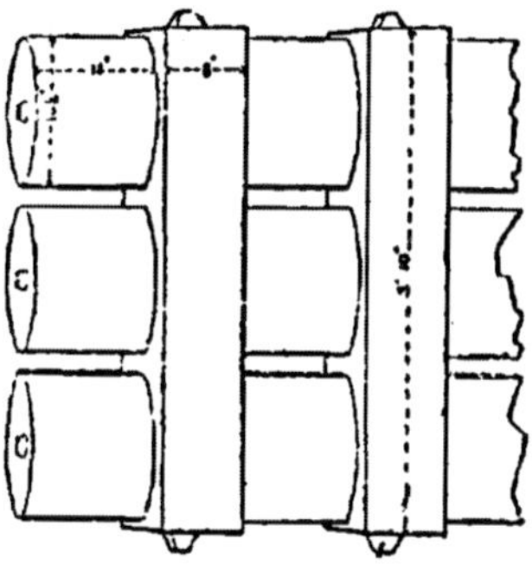

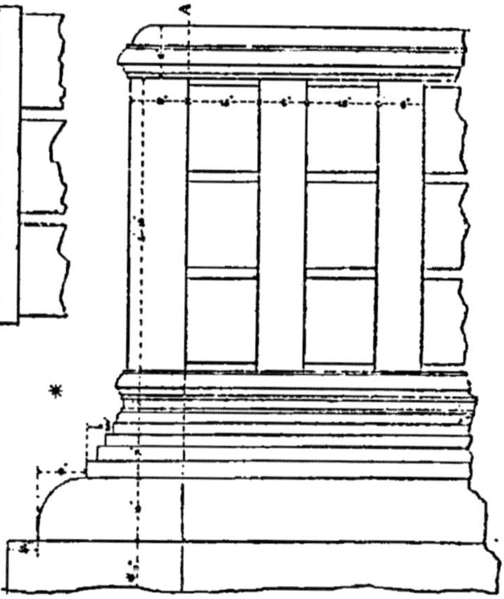

The lower plinth, * three-stepped (two, two and a quarter, two and three quarter inches), is seven inches in depth, the basement eight inches, and the socle nine inches—all cut on their upper surface with a half inch set to prevent the members above sagging outwards. The entire railing rested on a stone foundation, and from ground to coping was seven feet six inches in height.

---

* After these drawings were made a later discovery showed that a second ovolo member should come in above the stepped plinth, cf. plate facing page 106.

"Comparing it with the best known Indian examples, it follows that at Buddha Gaya in being rectangular, therein differing from the Bharhut, Sanchi and Amaravati rails. In unsculptured bareness it resembles the railing round the Great Tope of Sanchi, but carries simplicity even further by square, in lieu of octagonal posts."

The late James Fergusson, the eminent authority on Indian architecture, states in his "Rude Stone Monuments" that "the architectural material of India was wood down to B.C. 250 or 300. It then became timidly lithic, but retained all its wooden forms and simulated carpentry fastenings down, at all events, to the Christian era. The rail at Sanchi, which was erected in the course of the two centuries preceding our era, is still essentially wooden in all its parts, so much so that it is difficult to see how it could be constructed in stone." This is interesting in connection with the railing discovered at Anuradhapura, which is in pattern almost identical with the one at Sanchi, but is of solid granite. Moreover, its age must be somewhere about the beginning of the Christian era.

The following is taken from Mr. Bell's later report on this site:—"Considerable progress has been made in the excavation of the site near Abhayagiri Dagaba where the Buddhist railing was discovered. The whole of the ground between the rail and the inner basement line of the build-

PORTION OF BUDDHIST RAILING RESTORED.

ing has been turned up to a depth of six feet or more. Most of the rails, coping, &c., were unearthed within this space.

"On the east face, since the guard-stones alluded to in the last report were found, some grand columns of quartz, but greatly disintegrated, and unfortunately broken into two or three pieces, have been brought to light. Like the granite pillars already described, these have octagonal shafts, but a variant form of capital. The necking of the column slides into the round by a triple astragal moulding, upon which rests a flattened cushion capital, circular, with a low abacus.

"Near these pillars was dug out a single step of the east stairway. This is ten feet in length, the tread slightly fluted with a shallow lotus boss at each end, and a third at the centre. The riser of the step, also fluted, has in a central panel a horse kneeling to the proper left. The step is broken across the centre, but is otherwise little damaged, and not much worn.

"Some broken statuary was also exhumed. A very dilapidated kneeling bull in two pieces; of the Buddha, a sedent image complete, but in two; the lower portion of a second resting on the coils of Muchalinda Naga Raja; and the mere trunk of a standing figure. The last has small holes bored into it at the neck, wrists, and ankles, showing that the head, hands and feet were originally joined on by iron or copper joggles.

The hands of the seated Buddhas are as usual placed in their lap, the back of the right hand resting on the left palm. But the crossed feet have been carved in an impossible position, a false perspective, intended to exhibit to distant view the *magul lakunu*, or sacred marks on the soles—a conventionalism (abandoned in later days) which necessarily detracts from the artistic finish of the figure, giving it a somewhat distorted appearance. All these are of quartz.

"Specimens of nails and bolts (iron and copper) with a small copper bell and an iron chisel were dug up at different points.

"Starting near the centre, the brick walls of what proved to be a small chamber, eight feet square, were soon exposed at a depth of three feet to four feet below the level of the stone pavement, which was laid down in the corridors of the pillared bulidings if not throughout it. Some two or three feet height of the chamber walls remain above a well-laid brick flooring outside. It was full of the fallen brickwork. When this débris had been cleared, in the centre was discovered a box-like receptacle, two feet square by one foot in height, divided into half-a-dozen irregular partitions by bricks set up endwise. The chamber may have been originally a relic chamber, and this smaller compartment the receptacle of the actual relics and the gems, &c., stored with them.

MONOLITHIC STATUE OF BUDDHA.

"From the chamber brick walls of the most solid construction, or narrow pavements, three feet in width, branch off in several directions, probably to form separate rooms or mark passages. The bricks are of the largest size yet found in Anuradhapura, eighteen inches by nine inches by three inches, of excellent quality, sharply edged and kiln-baked to perfection. Those of the chamber and inner receptacle are smaller, twelve inches by nine inches by two inches. No mortar was used the whòle being in puddle—a strong evidence of its antiquity.

"When clearing round the chamber wall a large quantity of coloured beads of all sizes were picked out. These beads vary in size, from two five-eighths of an inch in circumference to the finest 'dust' variety, almost too diminutive to thread. The predominant colour is pale green, after which comes blue, orange, dull red, and black in the order given. The larger beads, and the greater part of the smaller kinds (with an exception of an oblong seed-shaped pebble), are of glass more or less corroded: a few are of bone. Found with the beads and apparently buried with them was a quantity of zircon and dark red garnets with some calcite and quartz.

"As at the site of the ancient temple at Tiru-kétisvaram, near Mannár, besides beads, fragments of ancient glass, plain and coloured, were turned up; thick glass two and a half inches long, small bits of thin blue and white glass, one sixteenth and one thirty-second of an inch thick. To these should be added a large lump of beautiful translucent rock crystal, and two worked crystal fragments—one an hexagonal prism, two inches long by one inch in diameter (perhaps the kota or pinnacle of a crystal dagaba-shaped karanduwa) —the other, the moulded pediment to a small image, both broken.

"But perhaps the most unexpected find was an oblong four-sided dice complete, and pieces of another, both of calcined bone.

"The reasonable expectation of discovering a large assortment of ancient coins has not been realised. Fortunately a few unearthed possess a historical value, which will go far towards fixing the age of the brick building. The coins comprise a few punch-marked 'eldings,' the oldest form of coin currency met with in India; some copper coins of the Kurumbar or Pallawa kingdom (at their zenith between the fourth and seventh centuries); two ancient Singhalese coins—those oblong figured tablets or plaques hitherto found mostly in the Northern Province. Most noteworthy are two 'third brass' coins of the later Roman Empire.

"The profusion of stone pavement, basement slabs, pillars, ornamental bosses, &c., covering and inextricably running down into the unconnected brickwork below at all angles in baffling

GALGE, OR ROCK CHAMBER.

confusion, is almost certain evidence of a stone superstructure richly colonaded (to which the magnificent railing was a fitting frame) raised upon the ruins of a still earlier structure of brick. The natural impression to be gathered from the present stage of the excavation seems to point to the site marking the ruins of two periods—a brick era, before the employment of mortar, followed by an age of stone construction, here exemplified at its best. It may prove impossible, even when the site is embowelled to the lowest strata of débris, ever to lay down with confidence the plan of the building which once stood upon it. Certainly until excavation from end to end reaches to the very foundations it were useless theorising as to its constructive features, its object first and last, and the varied fortune to which the early simple brickwork and subsequent stone elaboration were subjected."

Since the above was written further progress in the excavation of this site has been made, and the restoration of the Buddhist railing has been to some extent carried out. Unfortunately, when I secured my photograph in January, 1896, the railing itself was not *in situ*, but portions of it were lying quite close to the pediment mouldings which, as may be seen in the Plate facing page 106 were partially restored. The Plate facing page 108 shows the complete restoration which has since been effected.

Our Plate which faces page 110 represents a colossal figure of Buddha. It is a monolith eight feet high and has probably been in the forest where we now find it for more than a thousand years. It stands upon three pillar stumps now buried. It is carved in very dark granite, and the surface is now quite black.

Our illustration facing page 112 represents a galgé, or hermit's cell, excavated out of the natural rock, with an outer wall of brick. This is a place of considerable interest. The rock, which is a huge hummock about one hundred and twenty yards long, bears signs of having been extensively quarried for other buildings. Wedge marks, as in our illustration, appear in many parts, giving indications of the manner in which the builders detached the huge monoliths found everywhere, and going far to prove that two thousand years ago they used a method which was introduced into Europe in the nineteenth century. "This 'rock-house' or cave," writes Mr. Bell, "was prepared for its hermit priests with considerable care. First, a slice thirty-four feet in width by thirteen feet six inches deep was wedged from the rock; then a further depth of ten feet smoothly scooped out in ovolo shape, the bellying roof being beautifully rounded. Finally, a substantial wall, two feet thick, of brick and puddle was probably run up to form the front and divide the interior space into three chambers. The centre

RUINS OF THE DALADA MALIGAWA.

cell, entered by a chastely moulded stone door (six feet six inches by three feet five inches), is sixteen feet seven inches in length and eight feet six inches in depth, with a maximum height of eight feet nine inches. At the left back corner a stone shelf was cut; on the right of the doorway is a bed, and at the back a long seat, both fashioned of clay. This cell has two small windows, now blocked. The two side cells are very cramped, being but five feet six inches by five feet three inches and six feet one inch in height and entered by low arches. A katare was cut above the cells to divert the drip. In front of them is a rock cistern, twenty feet by eight feet six inches, hollowed from the slab rock."

Near this cave ruins are very abundant; the basements of upwards of twenty buildings, several fine pokunas, and quite a forest of pillars are visible.

We have already referred to Kitsiri Maiwan I., who finished the great Jetawanarama begun by his father, Maha Sen. In the ninth year of his reign, A.D. 311, the famous tooth-relic of Buddha was brought to Ceylon by a princess who in time of war is said to have fled to Ceylon for safety with the tooth concealed in the coils of her hair. The Dalada Maligawa, or Temple of the Tooth, was then built for its reception within the Thuparama enclosure. The ruins of this famous temple are well worthy of inspection.

The building appears to have consisted of an entrance hall, an ante-chamber, and a relic-chamber. Our illustration shows the moulded jambs and lintel of the entrance to the ante-chamber still *in situ*. The principal chamber is interesting for its curiously carved pillars, the heads of which are worked into a design often supposed to represent the sacred tooth. At the principal entrance there is a handsome flight of stone steps, at the foot of which is a richly-sculptured moonstone and a dvarpal on either side. The origin of the Perahara festivals, still held annually at Kandy,* dates from the erection of this temple from which the tooth was upon festival occasions borne through the streets of Anuradhapura on the back of a white elephant which was always kept at the temple for the purpose. During the invasions of the Malabars, when the temple was more than once destroyed, the sacred relic was on several occasions removed for safety and thus preserved, but at length, in the fourteenth century, it was seized and carried off to India. The Singhalese king Parakrama Bahu III., however, by proceeding to India successfully negotiated its ransom and brought it back again. There is a story of its having been taken and destroyed by the Portuguese at a later date, and although Europeans consider the evidences of this final mishap as historical,

* See the Author's "Picturesque Ceylon," Vol. ii.

REMAINS OF AN ANCIENT STREET.

the natives are satisfied that the original relic still exists in the temple at Kandy and regard it with the greatest veneration.

As we wander from one part of the sacred city to another and inspect remains which suggest a past of such grandeur and prosperity it is somewhat depressing to notice the squalid appearance of the modern native dwellings and their inhabitants. Although much has been done of late years to improve their lot by restoring means of cultivation and the fever demon has been banished by the removal of large tracts of jungle and forest, still the sight of the mud dwellings roofed with leaves and sticks amidst the signs of former magnificence gives rise to serious reflections. For the most part the miserable remnant of the native population live only on kurrukan, something like millet, not being even able to afford rice.

The native annals give many particulars of the streets of the ancient city, but considering how deeply buried are the foundations of buildings traces of the streets are difficult to find. There is, however, one of considerable interest at Toluwila, a couple of miles east from the centre of the city (Plate facing page 116). Here for several hundred yards the way is paved and on either side there are mouldings and copings. At intervals where the road rises and falls there are flights of steps, at which points there were probably some buildings. In the vicinity there are a good many indications of dwellings and a small dagaba. It is very likely that this was within the sacred part of the ancient city.

We have visited those architectural remains of Anuradhapura which have been reclaimed from the dense forest, but the greater part of the city still lies entombed. When in the twentieth century the whole province shall have been restored to the prosperity that certainly awaits it and the work of the archæological commissioner shall have borne full fruit, the contents of this volume will be an insignificant portion of the information available. At present we depart from the city with a feeling that we have touched only the fringe of a great and interesting subject.

MODERN NATIVE DWELLING.

CHAPTER V.

SIGIRI.

HITHERTO we have kept to the beaten tracks of travel but we now enter upon the more adventurous part of our journey which may be considered to begin with our visit to Sigiri. The historic interest which attaches to this lonely crag centres in the story of the parricide King Kasyapa, who after depriving his father Dhatu Sen of throne and life, sought security by converting this rock into an impregnable fortress. Although it has been said that Sigiri was a stronghold in pre-historic times, we have no account of it earlier than the time of Kasyapa, the particulars of whose reign related in the Mahawansa are considered specially reliable as being written by the Buddhist monk Mahanamo, an eye witness of the troublous times that he describes. It is, moreover, the only contemporary account of Sigiri that has come to light.

We cannot, therefore, more effectually stimulate our interest in this remarkable fortress than by recounting the story of outrage and cruelty which led to its adoption as a royal residence and its adaptation as a tower of defence. The actors in this tragedy, so thoroughly illustrative of the fiendish cruelty native to the Singhalese princes of that age, were king Dhatu Sen, who ascended the throne A.D. 463; his two sons Kasyapa and Moggallana; his only daughter; his uncle and our chronicler Mahanamo; and his nephew who was his commander-in-chief.

Dhatu Sen who was a scion of the line royal, had during his youth lived in retirement in consequence of the supremacy of the Tamil usurpers during the period from A.D. 434 to A.D. 459. Educated by Mahanamo he entered the priesthood, but upon reaching man's estate the oppression of the alien rulers, their devastation of the temples, and the prospect of a mixed and hybrid race, called him from a life of contemplation. Believing that his country was in danger of being lost for ever to the Singhalese, he resolved upon a desperate effort to recover the throne. In this he eventually succeeded, and after the complete extirpation of the invaders he applied himself to re-establish peace throughout the island and to restore the old religion to its former pre-eminence. Those of the nobles who had during the usurpation formed alliances with the Tamils were degraded to the position of serfs on their own land, but all who had remained steadfast in their devotion to their

SIGIRI.

country were called to honour, and more especially the companions of his adversities.

He now applied himself as vigorously to the arts of peace as he had to those of war. He founded hospitals for the halt and sick, constructed a large number of reservoirs in districts that had long been neglected, founded many new monasteries, restored and re-decorated all the chief religious edifices, devoting his private treasures and his large store of jewels to the re-adornment of statues that had been desecrated and despoiled. "Who can describe in detail all the good deeds that he has done?" says the Mahawansa.

We learn, however, that these great virtues were counterbalanced to some extent by a disposition to cruel revenge. We are told that having an only daughter dear to him as his own life he gave her in marriage to the commander-in-chief of his army. The marriage was not happy, and it soon reached the king's ears that his daughter had been ignominiously and undeservedly flogged by her husband. Dhatu Sen thereupon ordered the culprit's mother to be stripped and put to death with great cruelty. But this barbarous act soon brought its retribution. The son-in-law was now the aggrieved person and at once conspired to dethrone the king. This he accomplished by the corruption of Kasyapa. The people were gained over and the king seized and cast into chains. In vain Moggallana endeavoured to oppose his brother's treachery; he could only seek refuge in flight to India. The next move of the outraged son-in-law was to persuade Kasyapa that his father had hidden his treasures with intent to bestow them on Moggallana. Kasyapa thereupon sent messengers to his father who was in prison to demand of him where the treasures were concealed. Dhatu Sen saw in this a plot against his life, and resigning himself to his fate, said: "It is as well that I should die after that I have seen my old friend Mahanamo once more and washed myself in the waters of Kalawewa." * He then told the messengers that if Kasyapa would allow him to be taken to Kalawewa he could point out his treasures. Kasyapa, delighted at the prospect, sent the messengers back to his father with a chariot for his conveyance to Kalawewa. While on the journey the ill-fated king ate rice with the charioteer, who showed great compassion for him.

Upon arriving at Kalawewa he derived great solace from the interview with his old friend Mahanamo. He bathed in the great reservoir and drank of its waters; then pointing to his friend Mahanamo and to the waters around turned to his guards and said: "These are all the treasures that I possess." When they heard these words they were filled with wrath and immediately

---

* The immense artificial lake referred to on page 30 and the greatest work of this monarch.

conveyed him back to his son Kasyapa who, handing him over to the chief of the army, ordered his execution. He was now doomed to suffer the worst death that his arch-enemy could devise. After heaping insults upon him this fiend stripped him naked, bound him in chains, and walled up the entrance to his prison.

Kasyapa, having thus rendered himself unpopular by his crimes, and dreading an attack from his brother Moggallana, dared no longer to live openly in Anuradhapura and retired to Sigiri. The perpendicular sides of this rock made it impossible to climb, but Kasyapa by a clever device carried a spiral gallery around it gradually rising from base to summit. He next surrounded the rock with a rampart of great strength within which he collected all his wealth and treasure and set guards over them. He then raised a splendid palace and other buildings needful for the seat of government. Here he lived in great luxury. But in spite of all distractions he soon began to repent of the crimes which had placed him on the throne, and in true Buddhist fashion endeavoured to escape the meed of unfavourable transmigration by acts of merit such as the building of monasteries and the granting of lands for the support of the priesthood. Not less oppressive than the dread of his next life was the fear of retribution at the hands of his brother Moggallana, who at length invaded the island at the head of an overwhelming force. The two armies encountered each other "like two seas that had burst their bounds," and in the great battle that ensued Kasyapa, on coming to a deep marsh, caused his elephant to turn back so that he might advance by another direction. His followers interpreting this as a sign of flight broke in headlong rout, and Kasyapa committed suicide on the field. Having thus prepared ourselves with its history, we now proceed to the rock itself and the remains that are still extant. At Dambulla we provision one of our bullock-carts for the day and send it on six miles to the small village of Inamalawa, which marks the first stage of our journey to Minneria which we hope to reach the next night. At daybreak we drive to Inamalawa where we branch off through the jungle by a path too rough for springs but practicable for the bullock-cart although exceedingly difficult in places. The path is very picturesque, and the jungle gay with birds of brightest plumage and alive with wild animals. Troops of monkeys are frequently seen and jackals here and there put in an appearance.

At length after about six miles of this path we emerge into the open and of a sudden Sigiri appears rising abruptly from the plain. An artificial lake, formed under the south side of the rock, helps to form a striking picture (see Plate facing page 120). There are traces of massive stone walls enclosing about fifty acres

REMAINS OF THE GALLERIES OF SIGIRI.

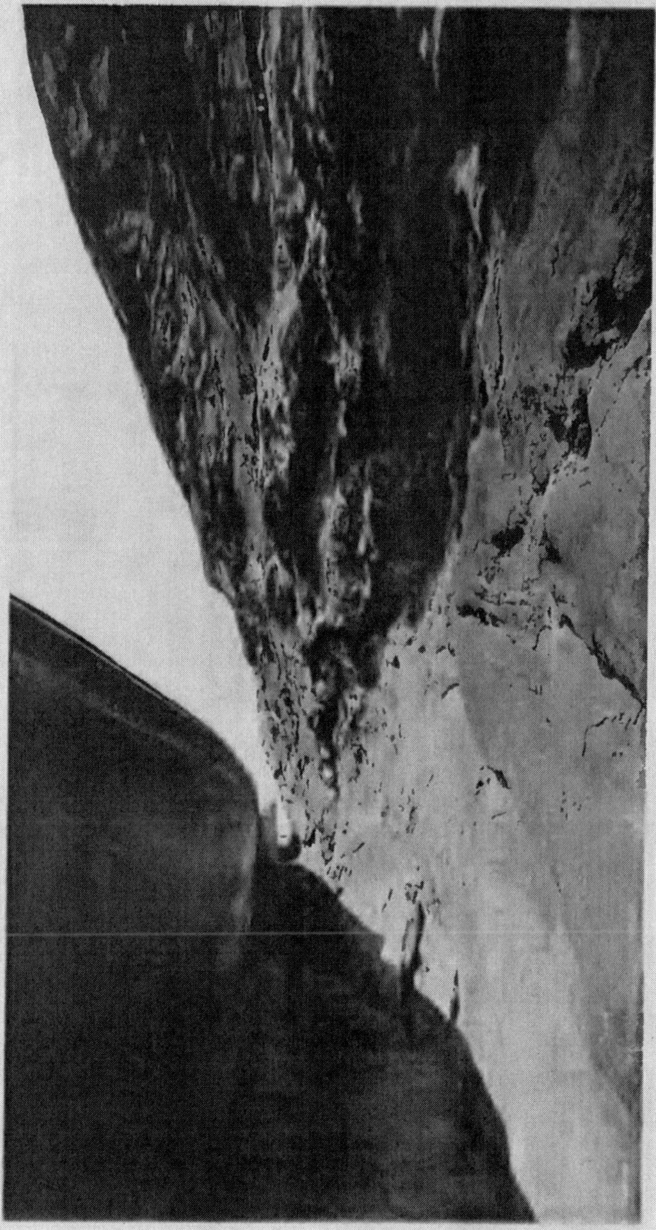

IN THE GALLERY OF SIGIRI.

round the base of the rock and forming the first line of defence. Upon a nearer approach we observe that terraces were formed on the slopes which lead to the perpendicular side of the rock; they are faced with stone and were doubtless constructed for purposes of defence. Here and there huge boulders have been carved into foundations for halls, and into luxurious baths. Mr. H. C. P. Bell, who is now engaged in the exploration, tells us of "scores of boulders, large and small, marked by grooves and mortice holes innumerable, that formerly held walls and pillars of the city buildings."

We have read in the story of Kasyapa of the spiral galleries which were carried to the summit of the rock. We now see in our illustrations parts of their remains. The Plates facing page 124 show the entrance to the gallery, the wall which enclosed it, and an inside view. The stairway from the terraces to the gallery has quite disappeared and the latter is now reached by an easy climb aided by the handrail and ladder which have been recently affixed.

The wall which will be noticed is about nine feet high, and was built on the edge of the terrace, so that persons within the gallery would have a sense of perfect safety, and, in fact, would be secure from the missile of any enemy. This wall is coated with chunam, a very hard cement, susceptible of a polish equal to that of marble, and it retains its smooth surface to this day although it has been exposed to the monsoons of fifteen centuries.

Those who have ascended this rock in modern times are few, for its galleries in most parts have entirely collapsed. The feat was a most dangerous one until an iron handrail was fixed by the government department of public works.* Even now in many parts a slip would mean instant death; but a few years ago the adventurous spirits who climbed this rock—and some half a dozen Englishmen are known to have done so—had to walk along six-inch grooves on the bare face of the cliff. This, I believe, would only be possible to the barefooted, and even then exceedingly dangerous. Moreover, there were other risks than slipping. The rock is noted for its colonies of bees, with an intensely painful and poisonous sting, which frequently attack and even disable the coolies at work upon the excavations. An assault by a hive of these when upon the six-inch ledge would certainly mean a fall down a sheer precipice of two or three hundred feet.

Forty-five feet above the gallery illustrated by our Plates facing page 124 there is a sort of pocket or shallow cave with some remarkable frescoes on its walls. They represent groups of

* This 2 feet high rail was so dangerous that the Architectural Survey has since erected a 5 feet rail with diagonal bars between standards.

COPYING THE FRESCOES OF SIGIRI.

females, probably queens and their attendants, and the colouring is still marvellously fresh and bright. This place is accessible only by means of a ladder hung on stays driven into the face of the rock, but the figures and the colouring can be seen very clearly by means of a field glass from the terraces below.

Mr. A. Murray ascended to the frescoes in 1889, and the careful crayon drawings that he made in colours like the originals may be seen in the Colombo Museum. He says "the freshness of the colouring is wonderful; and it is curious that green predominates, a colour rarely, if ever, used by native artists of the present day. In some portions of the roof that are more exposed to the elements the plaster has fallen away, affording a fair indication of the method by which it was attached to the rock. This was first chiselled to a fairly smooth surface, then a layer of finely tempered clay, mixed with rice husk and straw applied half an inch thick, and over this an equal thickness of lime mortar worked to an exceedingly smooth surface, upon which the paintings are executed."

In 1894 the Government archæological commissioner, Mr. Bell, took the risk of a climb to the summit by means of the ladders and the shallow rock grooves already referred to in order to gain a notion of the amount of work that would be necessary to fully complete the exploration. Since that time much has been done in clearing and excavating, and Mr. Bell has published an interim report of his operations, in which, referring to the summit, he says:—

"Excavations were started from the head of the steps which still mark the point where the 'gallery' reached the summit at the north-east edge of the rock. Progress was necessarily slow. The intense—almost unbearable—heat on the exposed and shadeless rock; only impure water from the pokuna to slake thirst; and an unusual depth (fifteen feet in places) to deal with of caked brick and stone débris, held together by tree roots, all rendered the daily task no light one.

"It soon became patent that we had to face ruins of at least two periods. Walls were found to run over walls, pavement above pavement, and stairs below stone ramps. I therefore deemed it advisable to sink the trenches down to the bare rock in most cases. As, too, the internal arrangement of rooms varied, every wall had to be followed along its inner as well as its outer face. Further, the certainty that buildings, passages, &c., covered the entire summit to the very edge of the cliff all round made it necessary to carry every basketful of earth, &c., to the eastern verge and throw it to spoil below.

"Broadly speaking, the buildings (so far as can at present be judged) seem to have contained spacious rooms separated by passages paved with

EXCAVATIONS ON THE SUMMIT OF SIGIRI.

quartz flags and united by quartz stairs—quartz everywhere—a striking feature of the Sigiriya ruins. One boldly-carved asanaya (nine feet ten inches by four feet six inches) or throne, hewn out of the mahá-gala (the gneiss rock core), has been exposed. It fronts east, and lies at the foot of the high ground west of the area excavated. A little useful work was also done near the south-west edge. The cistern sunk here into the solid rock, measuring thirteen feet two inches by nine feet ten inches and eight feet six inches in depth, was cleared of some seven feet of brick and mud, and scrubbed clean for future use, the ground round about being dug up and levelled off to prevent the wash of the rains finding its way again into the cistern."*

We shall not trespass further into the region of Mr. Bell's recent discoveries at Sigiri, it being our object to call attention to his brilliant work rather than discuss it in detail.

Our visit to Sigiri results in the very agreeable feeling that we have seen one of the most fascinating and romantic spots that the old-world scenes of any country can afford. The warm red tones of its cliffs, the beautifully worked quartz stairs of its ruined galleries and terraces, the picturesque lay of its massive ruins, the

* Since the first edition of this book was published, in 1897, these excavations have been completed; and the courtyards, passages and numerous apartments have been laid bare as seen in the plate facing page 128.

grandeur of the forest which surrounds it, and the waters of its lake, with the dark and mysterious reflections amidst the lotus leaves that o'erspread the surface, combine to form an impression that will never fade from the memory.

CHAPTER VI.

MINNERIA.

FROM Sigiri we retrace our steps through the forest to Inamalawa and drive thence to Habarane, which is six miles further north on the main road to Trincomalee. Here the comfortable quarters which we find at the rest-house are the more welcome after the toil of our visit to the rock fortress. It is indeed a surprise to find in that wild and sparsely inhabited part of the country such a clean and well appointed little bungalow for the use of travellers, and our satisfaction is none the less upon discovering that it is in charge of a clever servant who is an excellent cook. Having sent forward notice of our coming, upon our arrival at 8-30 p.m. we are punctually served with a dinner beyond reproach. No doubt hunger is an admirable sauce, and we arrive with a good supply, but still we are of opinion that the fare is better than the ordinary traveller could reasonably expect. These little details of the comfort afforded to visitors by the very practical provisions of the Government are not without interest, and the blessings of wayfarers are showered daily on the providence of our rulers.

Upon leaving Habarane for the lake of Minneria and the ruined city of Polonnaruwa, we quit the main road and are cast upon our own resources. For a few miles a minor road which is in course of construction serves us, and we proceed easily enough until within two or three miles of Minneria, when we have to trudge through marshes, our visit being made at the end of the wet season.

Whatever the discomfort of this may be, we forget it at the first glimpse of the lake. No words can adequately describe a thing of such exquisite beauty. Killarney and other well-known beautiful expanses of water and woodland may be mentioned in comparison, but at Minneria there are many additional charms of which climate is not the least. The islands and woodlands unexplored for a thousand years are so thoroughly things of nature. Then the creatures everywhere add to the romance; the myriads of curious birds, many of great size and magnificent plumage; the crocodiles lazily basking upon the banks, and the spotted deer often darting across the open glades. Even the knowledge that the elephant, the bear, and the leopard, though out of sight, are present in large numbers, lends additional interest to a scene

MINNERIA.

which is beyond description.

We find a modest bungaletta commanding one of the finest views from the bund. It is unfurnished, but in it we take up our quarters for the night, our native servants cleverly rigging up stick bedsteads to keep us high above the floor, a necessary precaution for the avoidance of malarial fever. In such a climate protection from cold is unnecessary, but something more than a tent is advisable owing to the miasma from decaying vegetation.

There are no ruins of any importance to inspect in the neighbourhood of this lake, but the lake itself is so well worth seeing that we are glad to spend a night here both on our outward and return journeys. Its history, too, is of very considerable interest in connection with our subject generally. It is said to have been constructed in the third century by Maha Sen, to whom reference has been made at Anuradhapura. Its circumference is about twenty miles. The masonry and earthwork dams which were formed to divert the waters of the stream which fills it extend for many miles and average a height of about eighty feet.

Nothing occasions us greater wonder or more fully attests the enormous energy of the ancient kings than the construction of these giant tanks and the numerous smaller ones dependent on them, forming a system of irrigation that established plenty throughout large districts otherwise beyond the pale of cultivation. Such works were not confined merely to the northern plains which are now so sparsely populated, but extended over the whole country. Even in the mountains of the Central Province at an elevation of six thousand feet we find remains of masonry and earthworks which were designed to divert the streams and rivers to those plains which were subject to periodical drought. There is evidence everywhere of such feats of engineering skill in irrigation matters as would in these days be a matter of pride to any nation. How they were possible in early times is only to be understood by a complete grasp of the conditions of government under which the ancient race existed.

There was undoubtedly a dense population under obligation of free labour in the king's service. They held their lands on condition of devoting a large share of their efforts to what was called rajah-karia—king's service. Under this tenure the monarch claimed free labour for the construction of irrigation works and the building ot temples and shrines. Such serfdom as this for the common good was no hardship in a country where agricultural pursuits, consisting chiefly of growing rice, could be carried on with a small demand on the labourers' time; where the tanks for storing and the channels for distributing the necessary water were so well made and so skilfully

RETURNING FROM POLONNARUWA AT EVENTIDE.

arranged that the precious fertilizer could be admitted to the fields at the exact time required and the surplus drawn off with equal ease at the proper moment. Such compulsory service was entirely for their own good, and its necessity is only too apparent at the present time when in a state of freedom it is found to be so difficult to restore the former conditions of health and prosperity; so much so that what has been done is, as we have hinted before, the result of a half-hearted compromise whereby the people have been enticed to give a certain amount of free labour in consideration of a greater contribution by the Government.

There are still lands belonging to Buddhist temples held by tenants on the condition of supplying labour for keeping the temples in repair, or of cultivating other lands to provide funds for the temple service; but the compulsory service for the tanks which fifty years ago might have been re-introduced to the salvation of the natives is now impossible, freedom having been prematurely granted to a people whose character is still such that they need a wise system of paternal control. That the provinces now lying waste will be restored to prosperity there is little doubt, but it will be done with greater difficulty and less speedily than might have been the case under the old régime. There are some five thousand tanks to be repaired and brought into a state of efficiency before this consummation can be reached; but the good work is proceeding.

At Minneria we find an engineer officer of the Public Works Department with a large staff of labourers at work upon the several ancient lakes which it is hoped will again serve the hundreds of smaller village tanks in the large district now centered by the ruins of the once mighty city of Polonnaruwa. To this gentleman, Mr. Weinman, we are indebted for valuable assistance without which we should be unable to reach the goal of our ambition. Not only had news that the jungle tracks were impassable and that the open country was all under water reached us from the headman of the district who had told us that it was impossible to reach Polonnaruwa at that time, but the drivers of the bullocks had heard of the prevalence of the cattle disease and with the coolies were on the brink of mutiny. We were, however, determined to make the attempt, and our good friend the district engineer above referred to then lent us his aid in the shape of a further supply of coolies to replace the disaffected.

Once on the way the coolies became manageable enough. Our party may be seen by reference to the Plate facing page 134. The scene is one of the open spaces which occur at intervals to relieve the monotony of the jungle tracks through which the journey for the most part

EN ROUTE FOR POLONNARUWA.

has to be made. The rough nature of these tracks may be gathered by reference to the Plate facing page 136, where one of our baggage carts seems to require the services of Hercules. Shouts of "thalu, thalu" (lift, lift) from the coolies ring through the forest as they haul the cart bodily out of the mud holes. We are struck with admiration and surprise at the power and pluck of the little bullocks, who after having fallen upon their knees in pulling their load up the steep of a torrent bed would never allow their humps to shirk the pole, but continued to push with all their might until the heavy weight behind them triumphantly emerged once more upon the level.

No less surprising is the skill of the drivers, whose keen watchfulness and ready resource are in request for three hours at a stretch, when every other minute promises an inevitable upset; at one moment they encourage their "steeds" to charge a trunk hurled across the path by some freakish elephant, and with resistless force the wheels strike and jump the obstruction; at another they crash down a steep incline amidst boulders of rock and through a stream of doubtful depth. Only, however, when the courageous little animals get literally wedged in some crevice do the eighteen coolies render any but lip service, and supplement their war whoop by real lifting.

Thus for about twelve miles we proceed in

the direction of Polonnaruwa, at a pace not exceeding one mile and a half an hour. For the most part the tracks which we follow lie through dense forests, but the journey is by no means monotonous. Apart from the incidents connected with our baggage transit there is sport to be had on the way. Spotted deer frequently bound across our path; large grey jackals put in an occasional appearance; the small black bear is there in goodly numbers; while elephants excite our wonder and curiosity at frequent intervals by their noiseless gliding off upon winding our approach, leaving evidence of their flight in fresh footprints in the soft earth. We seldom see a herd although many are near us, and if we are curious as to the size of individuals we have to content ourselves with measuring the diameter of their footprints—"ex-pede Herculem."

At one point of our journey we come across some hunters of the Afghan race surrounded by their captives recently taken and still bound as shown in our Plate facing this page. The Afghans who may be seen in the picture standing by their hut in the jungle have come to catch and export elephants to their own country. They are allowed to do this upon paying the Ceylon Government ten rupees for each elephant caught and a royalty of two hundred rupees for each one exported. There is a steady demand for

ELEPHANT HUNTERS AT POLONNARUWA.

them to supply the courts of the rajahs in India, and 'the enterprising Afghan is the man who does the business although he does not actually effect the capture. His method is to temporarily establish himself in some district where herds of elephants are known to be, and engage a party of Singhalese to capture them under his instructions. The Afghan alone carries a gun while the Singhalese are provided with ropes made from the fibre of the Kitool palm. They hide themselves near some spot where a herd is likely to come, and upon its arrival the Afghan fires off his gun merely to alarm the game. A stampede ensues and the Singhalese lasso them as they bolt. The noose flies round the leg of the beast, and with wondrous celerity the other end of the rope is coiled round the nearest large tree, and the elephant is left there until thoroughly subdued.

We are now within two miles of the ancient city, and our bullock drivers refuse to proceed further, but we are determined to reach it in spite of every discouragement from all manner of persons acquainted with the district. including the Dissawe or headman who resides there. We argue that where carts had been carts might go again, but we are met by the reply that the rains have been greater than for years and the country is therefore impassable. We then resolve to leave the carts and proceed on foot, the coolies carrying our baggage on their heads. We are told that the journey is possible for barefooted coolies, but that no Europeans can walk through the mud and water. However, we proceed and even enjoy the novel experience, though we arrive only just in time to save being caught by the darkness.

No one could be more astonished at our arrival than the Dissawe, Mr. Gabriel Jayewardene, who had in several letters cautioned us against attempting to come before the wet season was quite over. His surprise did not affect the warmth of his welcome, and we were the first visitors for two years. He placed at our disposal a little bungalow in a lovely position on the bank of the Topawewa, the principal lake of the old city. The bungalow was empty and slightly out of repair, but we were so elated at the completion of our journey that we did not criticise the sumptuousness of our shelter and proceeded to make ourselves happy upon the bare floors; but the Dissawe soon laid us under further obligation by supplying us with tables, chairs, and fresh milk, besides offering for the morrow his services as cicerone.

JETAWANARAMA AT POLONNARUWA.

CHAPTER VII.

POLONNARUWA.

POLONNARUWA had been a place of royal residence in the palmiest days of the older city, but it was not till the eighth century that it was adopted as the seat of government. The decay of Anuradhapura had been creeping on ever since the days of Kasyapa and the fortification of Sigiri. Internecine war fostered by rival branches of the royal house, no less than the interminable struggles with the Tamil invaders, hastened its downfall. The history of the sixth and seventh centuries is a story of bloodshed and anarchy; the murders of a dozen kings, conspiracies, and the assassination of high and low, made violent death an everyday occurrence; wholesale emigration set in; cultivation was interrupted and buildings and irrigation works alike were destroyed or neglected. At length the Tamils, taking every advantage of internal dissention among the natives, so strengthened their position in and around Anuradhapura that the only means of the Singhalese government retaining any pretence of power lay in retiring before them. These circumstances led to the establishment of Polonnaruwa as the capital and the fate of Anuradhapura was sealed, for when abandoned to the Tamils its debasement and ruin were assured. Unfortunately they were the worst type of conquerors. While overthrowing the Singhalese authority they made no attempt to introduce any order of their own, but rather encouraged and abetted every lawless effort at destruction. No wonder then at the spectacle of ruin and desolation presented by Anuradhapura after a few years of Tamil dominion.

The new capital, however, soon made amends, and grew with amazing rapidity until in its religious buildings, its royal palaces, its lakes and gardens, it eclipsed the older city in splendour as it did in extent. It was not, however, to remain long in tranquility. The Tamils soon made their way thither and the old struggle was repeated. Sometimes under a strong native king religion flourished and a spell of general prosperity was experienced, only to be followed by a period of disaster and destruction.

That the Singhalese should have been able notwithstanding this constant disquiet to build and maintain a city of such unrivalled wealth, beauty, and power, is proof enough of the splendid qualities of the race. For one century only, however, during the Polonnaruan epoch did they have a fair opportunity of exercising

JETAWANARAMA (FROM THE NORTH).

JETAWANARAMA (FROM THE SOUTH-WEST).

their natural faculties to full advantage. What they needed were freedom from the harassing incursions of marauders and a cessation of domestic rivalry amongst their rulers. These they obtained about the middle of the twelfth century, when there arose a genuine hero who commanded the allegiance of all his subjects. This monarch, Parakrama the Great, not only regained possession of the whole of the country by expelling the Tamils and quieting all disaffection, but even invaded India and other more distant countries. Under his rule the city of Polonnaruwa reached the zenith of its greatness, and we shall best gather the story of the desolate but impressive remains that we are about to visit by a review of Parakrama's reign as related in the Mahawansa.

We may at once say that the reader need not regard either the noble qualities or the innumerable great works which the historian assigns to this monarch as one whit extravagant or romantic, as they are fully attested by existing evidence.

In his youth we are told he was quick in the attainment of arts and sciences, and by the help of a higher wisdom he perfected himself in the knowledge of laws, religion, logic, poetry and music, and in the manly arts of riding and the use of the sword and the bow. He seems to have studied the arts of peace equally with those of war, and it is remarkable that even before he had entered upon the campaigns that were to bring the whole country under his dominion he formed his plans for restoring prosperity to the soil. In his first speech to his ministers he is reported to have said: "In a country like this not even the least quantity of rain water should be allowed to flow into the ocean without profiting man. . . . . Remember that it is not meet that men like unto us should live and enjoy what has come into our hands and care not for the people. Let there not be left anywhere in my kingdom a piece of land, though it be of the smallest dimensions, that does not yield some benefit to man."

To strengthen his hand before he entered upon the conquest of the rebellious tribes he arranged for the residence in his own palaces of the youth of all the noble families that they might grow up "familiar with the service of kings and become skilled in managing horses and elephants and in fencing."

Finding the wealth that he had inherited insufficient for the prosecution of his plans, he devised means of filling his treasury without oppressing the people. He increased the export of gems, and placed trustworthy officers over the revenue. And in order that the efficiency of his army might be improved he instituted mock

THUPARAMA AT POLONNARUWA.

battles, and personally selected the most dexterous for places of honour in the field.

When every department was perfect and his materiel of war prepared, having reviewed his army, he entered upon a series of contests with the various chieftains who still held possession of the greater part of the country. We pass over the particulars of the battles that he fought and won, our purpose being rather to follow the fortunes of the royal city.

When the various pretenders and disaffected tribes had been subdued or won over, as much by admiration of the great Parakrama as by the force of his arms, he submitted to a second coronation, which is described by the historian in the following words:—"On that day the deafening sound of divers drums was terrible, even as the rolling of the ocean when it is shaken to and fro by the tempest at the end of the world. And the elephants, decked with coverings of gold, made the street before the palace to look as if clouds had descended thereon with flashes of lightning; and with the prancing of the steeds of war the whole city on that day seemed to wave even like the sea. And the sky was wholly shut out of sight with rows of umbrellas of divers colours and with lines of flags of gold. And there was the waving of garments and the clapping of hands. And the inhabitants of the city shouted, saying, 'Live! O live! great king!' And there was feasting over the whole land, which was filled with arches of plantains intermingled with rows of flower-pots; and hundreds of minstrels chanted songs of praise, and the air was filled with the smoke of sweet incense. Many persons also arrayed themselves in cloths of divers colours and decked themselves in ornaments of divers kinds; and the great soldiers who were practised in war, mighty men, armed with divers kinds of weapons, and with the mien of graceful heroes, moved about hither and thither like unto elephants that had broken asunder their bonds.

"By reason of the many archers also, who walked about with their bows in their hands, it seemed as if an army of gods had visited the land; and the city with its multitude of palaces, gorgeously decorated with gold and gems and pearls, seemed like unto the firmament that is studded with stars.

"And this mighty king, with eyes that were long like the lily, caused many wonderful and marvellous things to be displayed, and adorned himself with divers ornaments, and ascended a golden stage supported on the backs of two elephants that were covered with cloth of gold. And he bore on his head a crown that shone with the rays of gems, like as the eastern mountain beareth the glorious and rising sun. And casting into the shade the beauty of spring by the strength of his own beauty, he drew tears of

ENTRANCE TO THE THUPARAMA AT POLONNARUWA.

joy from the eyes of the beautiful women of the city. And he marched round the city, beaming with the signs of happiness, and, like unto the god with the thousand eyes, entered the beauteous palace of the king."

Peace being established and the ceremony of the second coronation over, Parakrama applied himself at once to the advancement of religion and the welfare of the people. Buddhism had been riven to its very core by heresies and distracted by the disputes of its various fraternities; the great families had been ruined and scattered; crowds of poor were starving without any regulated means of relief; and the sick were absolutely uncared for. The king first brought about a reconciliation of the rival religious brotherhoods, a task in which his predecessors had for centuries failed, and which cost him more labour than the re-establishment of the kingdom. He erected alms-halls in every quarter of the city, making them beautiful with gardens, and endowing them with every necessity for the poor. He next built hospitals for the sick, in whom he took great personal interest, being himself a skilled physician. These were equipped with a staff so ample that no sick person was at any moment left without an attendant; and the king himself was their visitor, showing great pity and enquiring fully of the physicians as to their manner of treatment, ofttimes administering medicine with his own hands. Thus did his great natural kindness of heart endear him to the people.

Having secured the happiness of his people so long oppressed, he proceeded to enlarge and adorn the famous city of Polonnaruwa. With a keen determination that the works upon which he was about to spend great treasure should not suffer the fate of those of his predecessors which were so frequently plundered by the invader he turned his attention especially to the question of fortifications. He placed a chain of massive ramparts around the city and within this three lesser walls. There is not much doubt of the existence of these, and their eventual discovery will be a subject of great interest to future explorers.

Although Parakrama is credited with such genuine solicitude for his people that his memory even now is greatly revered, he was not less mindful of his own temporal comforts. He built for himself the Vejayanta, a palace of great splendour. It had seven stories, and its thousand rooms were no less remarkable for the massive and beautiful pillars that supported the floors than its roof which was surmounted by hundreds of pinnacles wrought in precious metals. The furnishing was equally sumptuous, from carpets of great value to the tables inlaid with ivory and gold.

The religious buildings erected by him during

CURIOUS ROUNDED COLUMN AND RUINS.

his reign of thirty-three years were very numerous, and for the most part of colossal proportion. Amongst them as showing the king's toleration of all religious systems is mentioned one for "propitiatory rites to be performed therein by Brahmans"; as well as the circular house "where he himself might listen to the Játakas of Buddha, read by the learned priest who dwelt there."

Nor were places of entertainment omitted. He built theatres glittering with golden pillars and delighted the assemblage with paintings, representing scenes of their hero's exploits; halls of recreation in which it seemed "as if the hall of assembly of the gods had descended to the earth, and the manners and customs of the whole world had been gathered together into one place."

The native chronicle refers to a temple built in the reign of Parakrama for the relic of Buddha's tooth, but neither of the ruins yet discovered can be positively identified as the one mentioned. It is said to have shone with roofs, doors and windows of gold and countless works of art both within and without, and to have been ornamented with canopies of divers colours. "It was like unto the palace of the goddess of beauty, and shone with a lustre so great that all that was delightful on earth seemed to have been gathered together and brought into one place."

The Mahawansa has also many references to the pleasant parks and gardens of the city in which the ornamental baths so frequently met with amongst the ruins were a special feature. One of the gardens is said to have been famous for "a bathing hall that dazzled the eyes of the beholder, and from which issued forth sprays of water conducted through pipes by means of machines, making the place to look as if the clouds poured down rain without ceasing."

Most of the remains of the city thus nobly enriched by the greatest of Singhalese kings are buried beneath many feet of soil or hidden in the dense forest that has overgrown the many thousands of acres over which they extend; but by the assistance of our good friend the Dissawe and his peace officer we are enabled to find all those which have been made accessible. The dagabas have all the characteristics of their prototypes at Anuradhapura less the charm of greater antiquity, so we will not repeat descriptions already given, but merely remark that they are numerous and in some cases of enormous dimensions. We shall find more advantage in interesting ourselves in those ruins which are distinctly characteristic of the mediæval city.

First, let us glance at the Jetawanarama temple, perhaps the most imposing pile remaining (Plates facing pages 140 and 142). It is a building of one hundred and seventy feet in length with walls about

KOTUWA.

twelve feet thick and eighty feet high. Though built of red brick it appears to have been plastered with chunam, which still adheres in patches, as may easily be seen by reference to Plate facing page 140. This is a view from the east showing the entrance between the two polygonal turrets. The warm tints of the crumbling bricks interspersed with lighter patches where the polished chunam still remains have a pleasing effect in the masses of green forest around, the complete scene when suddenly bursting on the sight being perhaps the most impressive we shall meet with. The dilapidated figure of Buddha, sixty feet high, opposite the entrance, gives a crestfallen appearance to the whole. The exterior decoration of the building is distinctly Hindu in character, which is the more strange when we consider that the Jetavana, after which this temple and its adjoining monastery are supposed to be built, was the famous temple of Buddha himself. But the curious mixture of Hindu character with that which is purely Buddhist is a special feature of the Polonnaruwan buildings. The cause is rather difficult to decide. It may be due to the influence of the victorious Hindus who at intervals held the island during several centuries combined with the broad eclecticism of Buddhism, but it is a question too abstruse and speculative to enter upon here at length.

There are doubtless beneath the soil foundations of many noble buildings around this temple. The native chronicle refers to eight stately houses of three stories built for the priests, and for the chief priest a mansion of great splendour containing many halls and chambers, also seventy image houses of three stories, besides a great number of lesser halls and libraries.

The Thuparama illustrated by our Plates facing pages 144 and 146 is no less interesting and picturesque. It is an oblong brick building with a square tower. The walls are very massive, and for the most part quite five feet thick. It was to some extent explored by Mr. S. M. Burrows in 1886, and the following is an extract from his report to the Government:—"The entrance to and interior of this curious building was almost entirely blocked up with fallen masonry and other débris. This has been removed at a considerable cost of labour, for most of the fallen blocks of masonry were so large that they had to be broken up with the pickaxe before removal was possible. But the labour was well expended, for the inner and principal shrine is one of the very few buildings remaining to us in either capital with a perfect roof; certainly the only building of such a size, and it presents a very remarkable example of the dimensions to which the false arch was capable of attaining. The fragments of no less than twelve statues of Buddha (none

SAT-MAHAL-PRASADA.

quite, though some very nearly, perfect) were found in this shrine, while at the foot of the large brick statue of Buddha which stands against the western wall a large granite slab or stone seat ('gal-ásanaya') was uncovered, with an excellently preserved inscription running round its four sides."

The following is a translation of the inscription referred to:—

"His Majesty, Kálinga Chakrawarthi Parákrama Báhu, who was a descendant of the Okaka race, having made all Lanka's isle to appear like a festive island, having made all Lanka like unto a wishing-tree, having made all Lanka like unto an incomparably decorated house, having subjugated in war Sita, Choda, Gauda, &c., went to Maha Dambadiwa with great hosts; and seeing that because of his coming kings and others left their countries and came to him for protection, he treated them with kindness and stilled their fears; and having met with no rival after his landing in Dambadiwa, he erected pillars of victory, and again came to Lanka's isle. Lanka having been neglected for a long time, he erected alms-houses at different places throughout the whole of Dambadiwa and Ceylon; and on his return spent ever so much treasure on mendicants. Not being content with all this, he determined on a distribution of alms four times in every year, and by (giving) gold, jewels, cloth, ornaments, &c., having extinguished the poverty of the inhabitants of the world, and done good to the world and to religion, this is the seat on which he sat to allay body weariness."

The Thuparama is suffering greatly from the inroads of vegetation. Parasitic plants take root in the crevices, and growing into great trees rend the walls. Our Plate facing page 150 serves to show how they creep over the brickwork and push their way into great masses of masonry. This picture of a spot called Kotuwa, or the Fort, is introduced merely to show the disruptive effect of trees on the brickwork. The building may or may not have been a fort. Its massive walls, which are all that is left, have no doubt suggested the name.

The Sat-mahal-prasada, or palace of seven stories, is another building the origin of which is veiled in mystery. Statues ornament each storey, and there are traces of a staircase within, but it does not appear to lead to the summit, which can only be reached from without by means of ladders. There is an exterior flight of steps leading however only to the top of the first storey.

The most venerable of all the relics of Buddha, the tooth, experienced so many vicissitudes and translations during the Tamil wars that the stories of its various hiding places, and the temples built for its reception, as recorded in the ancient chronicles, are somewhat confusing. In the account of Parakrama's foundation at Polonnaruwa (see page 149) we read of the beautiful temple he built; and again very little later the historian tells of the temple built for it in the same city by Nissanka Malla, who came to the throne A.D. 1198, only two years after Parakrama's death. And as there are other allusions to the arrival of the tooth at Polonnaruwa at a later date, it may well be inferred that it was at various intervals removed for safety. It is curious, however, that both Parakrama and Nissanka Malla should have built magnificent temples for the same object about the same date, and to which of these kings to ascribe the building known as the Dalada Maligawa at Polonnaruwa, the remains of which present the most beautiful specimen of stone work

DALADA MALIGAWA AT POLONNARUWA.

yet discovered (see Plate facing page 154), it is difficult to decide. The Mahawansa says that Nissanka "built of stone the beautiful temple of the tooth relic," and what we see is generally attributed to him; but possibly the earlier description refers to the same building, although it is generally supposed that Parakrama's shrine was a curious and elaborate circular building known as the Wata Dágé, and that a second temple was built for the tooth by Nissanka.

It will be noticed from our Plate that the stone work is in beautiful preservation considering its age. The roof has gone, but the mouldings and toolings of the granite have scarcely suffered at all from their exposure of seven centuries.

One of the most interesting of the discoveries at Polonnaruwa is a rock temple with three colossal figures and a shrine carved out of one huge boulder of dark brown granite (Plate facing page 156). This is known as the Gal Vihara. In spite of appearances these figures are still part of the rock in which they were hewn. The work is very cleverly done, and especially the recumbent statue of Buddha, which is forty-six feet in length. The head rests upon the right hand supported on a bolster into which it sinks very naturally, suggesting nothing but perfect repose; the folds of the robe are also carved with equal fidelity. The erect statue is thought to represent Ananda, the favourite disciple of Buddha.

It is twenty-three feet high, and stands on a pedestal ornamented with lotus leaves. . Beyond this is the entrance to the temple itself, and within an altar and an image of Buddha in sitting posture, all carved out of the same rock in similar high relief. The shrine has been profusely decorated and coloured by modern devotees. At the farther end will be noticed a large sitting statue of Buddha, the figure alone being fifteen feet high. It is a most elaborate work, with a background of carved pagodas, and the pedestal is ornamented with a frieze of lions and quaint emblems. There is no doubt as to the date of this striking and curious specimen of rock temple, as it is referred to in the Mahawansa as the work of the great Parakrama.

A complete description of even those ruins that have been discovered in the explorations that have been made with such limited resources is beyond the scope of the present work. How many still lie hidden in the dense forest it is impossible to say, but when we look at the records of those only which were built during one or two of the most prosperous reigns we cannot help being impressed with the possibilities of the great "finds" that will be made when the whole province is again cleared and brought under cultivation. Then railways will convey thousands of visitors from every part of the world to these ancient cities which will surely find their rightful

ROCK TEMPLE AT POLONNARUWA.

place among the monuments of the world.

We must not take our leave of the Polonnaruwan remains without a glimpse at one which seems to deserve a parting glance. A walk of a little more than a mile along the lofty embankment of the Topawewa, one of the most remarkable instances of the highest art concealing itself, and more beautiful than ever now that it has been left for so many centuries to the great artificer, Nature, brings us to a large hummock of rock abruptly rising from the plain. In this rock is a striking statue of King Parakrama carved, like that of the recumbent Buddha, in the solid rock. (See Plate facing page 158). The monarch, who raised most of the temples and monuments of the city, stands with his back to his great works holding an ola, or palm leaf book, in his hands as if at the end of his glorious reign he had found in the study of the Buddhist scriptures his final consolation.

With the death of Parakrama in 1197 the power of the Singhalese nation began to decline. For a few years only at the beginning of the thirteenth century was the country again under capable government. The prosperity and wealth to which the city had attained only served to excite the rapacity of invaders. The Tamils, twenty thousand strong, under a chief named Magha took Polonnaruwa in the year 1215 and laid waste the whole country. "This Magha" says the Mahawansa, "who was like unto a fierce drought, commanded his army of strong men to ransack the kingdom of Lanka, even as a wild fire doth a forest. Thereupon these wicked disturbers of the peace stalked about the land hither and thither crying out boastfully, 'Lo! we are the gaints of Kerala.' And they robbed the inhabitants of their garlands and their jewels and everything that they had. They cut off also the hands and feet of the people and despoiled their dwellings. Their oxen, buffaloes, and other beasts they bound up and carried away forcibly. The rich men they tied up with cord and tortured, and took possession of all their wealth and brought them to poverty. They broke down the image houses and destroyed many cetiyas. They took up their dwellings in the viharas and beat the pious laymen therein. They flogged children and sorely distressed the five ranks of the religious orders. They compelled the people to carry burdens and made them labour heavily. Many books also of great excellence did they loose from the cords that bound them and cast them away in divers places. Even the great and lofty cetiyas they spared not, but utterly destroyed them, and caused a great many bodily relics which were unto them as their lives to disappear thereby. Alas! alas! Even so did those Tamil gaints, like the giants of Mara, destroy the kingdom and religion of the land. And then they surrounded the city of Polonnaruwa on every side, and took

STATUE OF KING PARAKRAMA.

Parakrama Pandu captive and plucked out his eyes, and robbed all the treasures that were therein with all the pearls and precious stones." *

* The quotations from the Mahawansa in this chapter have been taken from the translation of Mudaliyar L. C. Wijesinha.

CHAPTER VIII.

THE ROCK TEMPLES OF DAMBULLA AND ALUWIHARI.

IT remains now only to retrace our steps to Colombo, and to visit on the way the famous rock temples of Dambulla and the Aluwihari at Matale, which date from the first century B.C. In their natural state they were selected as hiding places by King Walagambahu upon his being driven by the Tamils from his throne at Anuradhapura. After fifteen years of exile he regained his throne, and in gratitude for the protèction they had afforded him transformed them into temples.

Those at Dambulla are a series of five natural caverns entered from a ledge near the summit of a huge boulder of dark gneiss five hundred feet high and two thousand in length. The ascent is made by a steep but picturesque stairway cut in the natural rock. At the top of this a landscape bursts into view that apart from the interest of the temples would well repay a more toilsome climb. Ranges of mountains stretch away over the Kandyan province in the dim grey distance;

the rock of Sigiri rises in solitary grandeur from the dense forest to the east; and beneath us lie the rice fields granted by the ancient kings as the endowment of the temples.

Our Frontispiece gives some idea of the formation of the ledge and overhanging rock above the entrances to the caves. It is, however, difficult to get a photograph at all owing to the short distance which it is possible to recede. This ledge where we see three monks standing extends only to the tree on the left and ends in a precipice. We see the rude entrances to the caves on the right. They are, of course, modern, and like all attempts at restoration in this period are totally out of character with the place. But the scene presented on entering is imposing, though weird and grotesque. We notice at once a strange mixture of Brahman and Buddhist images and pictures. Here is Vishnu in wood standing opposite to a colossal figure of Buddha recumbent in stone forty-seven feet long and carved out of the solid rock. As soon as the eye gets accustomed to the dim religious light we notice that the walls are highly ornamented, and we learn from the monks that some of the frescoes are nearly two thousand years old.

In another compartment called the Maha Vihara there is a statue of King Walagambahu, and upwards of fifty others mostly larger than life size, many being images of Buddha, though Hindu deities are not negelected. This cave is the largest and grandest of all. It is about one hundred and sixty by fifty feet, and at the entrance twenty-three feet high, the roof sloping gradually down as we go further into the chamber till at the back its height is but four feet. The student who is interested in the relation between Buddhism and Hinduism will remark a very curious blending of the symbols of both in the frescoes with which the walls and ceilings are literally covered. Not less noticeable are many historical scenes, among them the famous combat between King Duttha-gamini and the Tamil prince Elara, to which we have already referred. There are besides many quaint representations of earlier events, amongst which the most curious is perhaps the landing of the Singhalese under Prince Wijayo, B.C. 543. The size of the fish who are popping up their heads above the waves and menacing the ships is that affected by all the ancient hydrographers.

The other two chambers are of the same shape though smaller, and are furnished with a plentiful supply of objects of worship, from the usual cyclopean monolithic Buddhas to smaller images of the Hindu deities.

Few visitors enter these caverns without being greatly impressed by the strange and eerie sight which seems to increase as the eyes get more accustomed to the dimness, while some are even haunted by the memory of the uncanny vision.

There are many interesting inscriptions on the bare face of the rock, one of which is an ordinance that when absolute grants of land are made such dispositions shall not be recorded on palm leaves, which are liable to be destroyed, but shall be engraved upon plates of copper, to be imperishable through all ages. This ordinance is attributed to the great Parakrama, and it sometimes happens even now that a copper title-deed figures in the law courts of Colombo as evidence in disputed cases of ownership.

Leaving Dambulla we pursue our homeward journey for some thirty-five miles until just before reaching Matale we turn aside to the rock temple of Aluwihari, which claims our attention both as an extremely picturesque spot and one to which is attached considerable literary interest. We take to a jungle path off the main road till we come upon a flight of stone steps which lead to what appears to have been originally a cleft in the rock (Plate facing page 18.) On the left side runs a verandah, a modern tiled erection, which conceals the entrance to a cavern sacred as the scene of King Walagambahu's convention of monks in the first century B.C., at which were transcribed the sayings of Buddha hitherto preserved only by tradition. The object of the convention was, however, not confined to the mere committal to writing of the master's words but had in view also the provision of means of combating the heresy of the Abhayagiriya fraternity, which, as we have remarked in a previous chapter, was then causing serious trouble at Anuradhapura.

To the enlightened Buddhist this secluded and comparatively unpretending cavern must be of infinitely greater interest than the Temple of the Tooth or the Thuparama itself.

Protected by the verandah and painted on the exterior of the rock are some interesting frescoes with a striking resemblance in idea as well as in execution to the rude mediæval illustrations of the punishments awaiting the impious in a future state. Such representations are found in most Buddhist temples.

And now that we have made the round of the ruined cities we cannot but be painfully impressed with the meagre knowledge that is at present at our disposal. Only the merest fringe of this great subject has been touched. We have followed in the wake of pious devotees and of a sympathetic Government who have, no doubt, spent considerable sums in such work of renovation and exploration as has already been accomplished. But this is merely infinitesimal. The trackless jungle still covers the greater part of the huge cities of Anuradhapura and Polonnaruwa, while other remains of its glorious past are scattered here and there all over the island. The work of exploration proceeds slowly; more funds are

FRESCOES AT THE ALUWIHARI ROCK TEMPLE.

needed, and these can only be expected from Government sources. Not that the Buddhists of to-day are indifferent to the monuments erected by the piety of their forefathers. At the present moment a scion of the royal house of Siam is devoting a large fortune to the restoration of the Miriswetiya Dagaba at Anuradhapura; but it is hopeless to expect that the equally costly work of laying bare the buried remains can be carried out by the private enterprise of individuals.

Should it be the good fortune of this unpretentious account, of whose many imperfections no one is more conscious than the author, to arouse the interest of those to whom the ruined cities are unknown and to quicken that already existing, the object of this volume will be amply realised.

INDEX.

Abhayagiriya Dagaba, 91
„ „ Altars of, 92
„ Fraternity, 164
Aborigines, 32
Adam's Peak, 45
Agriculture in early times, 3, 4
„ Ideal condition of, 4
Aluwihari, cave-temple, 18, 163, 164
Ambustele Dagaba, 47
Ananda, Statue of, 155
Animals, Wild, 4
Antiquarian interest, 17
Anuradhapura, Inner city of, 11
„ Journey to, 13
„ View of, from Mihintale, 36
„ Decay of, 141
Arittha, 57
Asoka, 41, 57
Aryans, 32, 37

Basawak Kulam, 95
Batiyatissa, Statue of King, 72
„ festoons the Ruanweli Dagaba, 86
Reads, Discovery of ancient, 111
Bell, Mr. H. C. P. Explorations at Sigiri, 127
Benares, 37
Bimbisara, Conversion of, 38
Birds, 26
Bo-Tree, Sacred, 7, 56, 57
Botany, 31
Brazen Palace, 8, 64, 65, 66, 68, 69
Bricks, Peculiar shape of, 97
Buddha, Death of, 40
„ Visits to Ceylon by, 43
„ Relic of the collar bone of, 52
„ Statues of, at Ruanweli, 72
„ Colossal statue of, 114
„ Recumbent statue of, 155
„ Sayings of, first transcribed, 163

Buddhism, Its adoption by the Singhalese, 37
„ Principles of, 38
„ Its four dogmas, 39
„ in the time of Parakrama, 147
Buddhist Railing, 105
Bullock Carts, 14

Canopy, Stone, 103
Ceylon in early times, 2
Circular House, 149
Civilization, Dawn of, in India, 32
Clusters of Pillars, 87
Cobra, Buddhist legend regarding the, 5
Coins, Discovery of Ancient, 112
Communication, Want of, 16
Coolies on the march from India, 20
Crocodiles, 62

Dhatu Sen, King, 120
„ „ „ Murder of, 123
Daladá Máligáwa at Anuradhapura, 56, 115
„ „ at Polonnaruwa, 154
Dambulla, 21, 25, 124
„ Rock Temples at, 159
Dancing Halls, 8
Dutthagamini, King, 64
„ „ Fight with Elara, 64
„ „ Statue of, 73
„ „ Death of, 83
„ „ Dying wishes of, 85
Dvarpal at Maha Sen's Palace, 100
Dwellings, Native Modern, 117

Elara usurps the throne, 64
„ Tomb of, 65
Elephant Wall at Ruanweli Dagaba, 70
Elephants, Catching, 138, 139
Engineering skill in early times, 134
Etwehera Dagaba, 36
Explorations, Future, 156

Flowers, Culture of, 4
„ Use of, 10
Foundations of Shrines, 69
Frescoes at Sigiri, 127

Galgé, 114
Gal Vihara at Polonnaruwa, 155
Gems, Export of, 144
Giri, Island of, 44
Glass, Discovery of ancient, 111
Golden Age of Lanka, 1
Gotama chooses the life of a mendicant, 38
Greeks, Invasion of India by the, 40
Gregory, Sir William, 16

Habarane, 131
Health of inhabitants improving, 17
Heresy, Buddhist, 68
History of Remains, Authentic, 35

Inamalawa, 124, 132
Incidents of travel, 15
Information, Sources of, 2
Inhabitants, Destitution of, in modern times, 16
Inner City, 11
Inscriptions upon natural rocks, 6
Inscription of Nissanka, 73
Inscriptions, Old Singhalese, 76
Irrigation Works, 16
" " repairs to, 17
Isurumuniya Temple, 62
" " Bas Relief sculptures at, 63

Jetavana, 151
Jetawanarama at Anuradhapura, 95
" at Polonnaruwa, 130
Johannis, Ingenuity of, 23
Journey to Anuradhapura, 13
Jungle, Clearance of, 17

Kalawewa, 30
Kalawewa, Dhatu Sen's last visit to, 122
Kandyan District, 15
Kasyapa, King, fortifies Sigiri, 119
" " Suicide of, 124
Kekirawa, 26
Kitsiri Maiwan, 115
Kotuwa, 153
Kuttam-pokuna, 88
Kynsey, Dr. 17

Lakes, Artificial, 3
Language of the Singhalese, 33
Landscape, Beauty of, 3
Lion, Carving of, at Maha Sen's Palace, 99
Loha Pasada, 65

Magadha, 38
Magha, Polonnaruwa taken by, 157
Mahámégha Garden, 7
,, ,, Ceremony of dedication, 50
Mahanamo, 119, 122
Maha Seya Dagaba, 36
Maha Sen, 68
,, ,, Results of his recantation, 94
,, ,, Palace of, 98
Mahathupa, Ceremony of foundation, 78
Mahawansa, 33
Mahinda, 34, 37, 41, 42
Mahinda, Bed of, 48
Malaria, 21
Manufactures, 11
Mátalé, 13, 17
Mihintale, 19, 32, 35
,, Interesting features of, 46
,, The great Vihara at, 46
Minneria, 132
Moggallana, 120, 122, 123
Moonstones, 100
Murray, Mr. A. 127

Naga Pokuna, 47
Nagas, 45
Nalandé, 20
Nissanka, Inscription of, 74
Nissanka Malla, 154

Olas, Preservation of, 35
Ootooankande, 15, 27

Pandu-Orua, 56
Parakrama the Great, Accomplishments of, 143
,, ,, Speech to his Minister, 144
,, ,, Second Coronation of, 145
,, ,, Works of, 147
,, ,, Statue of, 157
Parangi, 16
Park-like scenery, 87

Pataliputra, 57
Peacock Palace, 93
Perahera, Origin of, 116
Pokunas, 10
Pokuna, Restored, 88
Polonnaruwa, Road to, 136
Polonnaruwa, Incident of journey to, 137, 138
 „ History of, 141
 „ Theatres at, 149
 „ Taken by the Tamils, 157
Potter, Native, 19
Provisions, 14

Queen's Pavilion, 100
Quinine, 21

Railing, Buddhist, 105
Raja-kariya, 5, 134
Ramparts at Polonnaruwa, 148
Resthouses, 22
 „ Fare at, 22
 „ Amusement at, 22
River courses, 3
Roads, 14
Route, 14
Ruanweli Dagaba, 69
 „ „ Objects of interest around, 72
 „ „ Foundations of, 76
 „ „ Relic Chamber of, 80

Sadhatissa, King, 68
Sakyans, 37
Sanchi, Buddhist railing at, 108
Sanghamitta, 57
Sardiel, 27
Sat Mahal Prasada, 154
Saunders, Sir Frederick, 28
Sidhatta, The Thera, 79
Sigiri, 119
 „ Gallery of, 123, 125
 „ Ascent of, 126
 „ Frescoes at, 127
Singhalese, conditions of existence of, in early times, 1
 „ Of what race were the, 32
 „ Early history of, 33
 „ Language of, 33

Singhalese, Conversion of, 43
" Qualities of the race of, 142
" Nation, Decline of, 157
Situation of Ruined Cities, 14
Steps, Height of, at Mihintale, 35
Streets in early times, 8, 11
Sumana, 44

Tamils, Debasement of Anuradhapura by the, 142
" Polonnaruwa taken by the, 157
Tanks now in working order, 17
Temple Lands, 135
Theatres, 8
" at Polonnaruwa, 149
Thuparama Dagaba, 53
" at Polonnaruwa, 152
" explored by Mr. S. M. Burrows, 152
Tirappanne, 26
Tissa, King, 41
" " Conversion of, 46
" " Monuments erected by, 49
Toluwila, Excavations at, 117
Tooth of Buddha, its arrival in Ceylon, 56
" " Ransom of, by Parakrama, 116
Tooth, Temple of the, 56, 115
Topawewa, 140, 157
Trees, 30
Trough, Ornamental Granite, 55

Vejayanta, The, 148
Visitors' Book at Dambulla, 22

Walagambahu, King, Deposition of, 90
" Vanquishes Dathiya, 91
" Hiding place of, 160
" His convention of monks, 163
Wata Dágé, 155
Water, 15
Ways and means for travelling, 13
Wealth in early times, 2
Wijayo, 34

Yakkas, 33
Yogi Stones, 102